Grammar In 60 Minutes!

The Ultimate Crash Course to Learning the Basics of English Grammar In No Time

By
Dagny Taggart

© Copyright 2014

All rights reserved. No portion of this book may be reproduced -mechanically, electronically, or by any other means, including photocopying- without the permission of the publisher.

Disclaimer

The information provided in this book is designed to provide helpful information on the subjects discussed. The author's books are only meant to provide the reader with the basics knowledge of the topic in question, without any warranties regarding whether the reader will, or will not, be able to incorporate and apply all the information provided. Although the writer will make his best effort share her insights, the topic in question is a complex one, and each person needs a different timeframe to fully incorporate new information. Neither this book, nor any of the author's books constitute a promise that the reader will learn anything within a certain timeframe. The expression "Grammar In 60 Minutes" is a mere orientation given the relationship between the amount of words on the book and the reading speed of an average (and above average) reader. Learning such a complex topic could potentially take much more considering each reader's circumstances.

Table of Contents

INTRODUCTION: Why You Can't Afford Not to Learn Grammar!

Parts of Speech (Nouns, Verbs, Adjectives)

Pronouns (Subject, Object, Possessive)

Verbs and Their Tenses (Present + Past + Future)

A Note on Irregular Verbs

Punctuation and Style (Do Not Miss Out On This!

Types of Sentences (Simple, Compound, Complex!)

Building a Strong Sentence, The Right Way!

Avoiding Common Errors (Capitalization, Homophones, Etc)

Do THIS to Write Better Sentences!

Notes on Good Writing (You Can Do It, Trust Me!)

Writing Formats (These Can Be Confusing…)

5 Amazing Grammar Websites to Supercharge Your Learning

Congratulations, You've Done It! - Where to Go From Here

Preview Of "Learn Spanish In 7 DAYS! - The Ultimate Crash Course To Learn The Basics of the Spanish Language In No Time"

About the Author

Dedicated to those who love going beyond their own frontiers.

Keep on traveling,

Dagny Taggart

INTRODUCTION
Why You Can't Afford Not to Learn Grammar!

So what's the big deal about grammar anyway? It's quite a big deal actually. You see people may say they don't judge others' writing, but they do. A poorly written memo or a report with subpar grammar can label an individual as uneducated. And though everyone makes mistakes, some grammatical mistakes can be worse than others. In fact, a poorly placed comma or incorrect word can completely change the meaning of a sentence. Don't believe me? Google "comma fails". Did you laugh at some of the horrible mistakes? Proper grammar allows writers to clearly communicate their meaning. Take a look at the following two sentences:

1. **Our new chef is inspired by baking nature and families.**

   Without commas, this sentence communicates that the chef bakes nature and families—as in he's chopping up fingers and turning them into cupcakes. And how exactly does one bake nature anyway? Poorly written sentences typically leave the reader in a state of utter confusion. This sentence implies the chef is likely deranged; unless this sentence is a tagline for a new horror movie, it's simply wrong.

2. **Our new chef is inspired by baking, nature, and families.**

   With commas, this sentence communicates that the chef finds inspiration through three different things: baking, nature, and families. This sentence simply makes sense. Not only does it make sense, but it reveals important details about the chef. First, he prefers baking. Second, natural items such as flowers, water, and forests inspire his culinary creations. Third, he considers families when cooking, so his dishes are likely both delicious and cost effective. Commas are important!

A lot of people feel intimidated by grammar…and rightly so; it's rather like learning a new language. Suddenly words like brackets, clause, conjunction, object, preposition, subject, and run-on rear their ugly heads and demand your attention. Grammar clearly has its own terms. The good news is that learning grammar rules is just like learning to walk: if you place one foot in front of the other eventually you'll master it. The trick is to keep trying. Watch other people use good grammar (read, read, and read some more). Try. Fall down. Get back up and try again. Eventually you'll run—your sentences will be perfect and others with poor grammar will envy you.

And another reason grammar is so important? In today's technological age, poor grammar can go viral instantly. Entire websites devotedly post grammatical errors for world-wide viewing. Your coworkers, family, and peers will judge you for constructing poorly written sentences. Learning proper grammar ensures that you'll be able to sidestep everything from minor ridicule to seriously embarrassing faux paus. So how can you avoid infamy? Learn the rules.

This quick grammar review covers the basics of what you need to know to write clear, concise, and meaningful sentences. The goal here is to give you the "nuts and bolts" of grammar: its key parts and how to use them effectively. We'll start with the building blocks of language, parts of speech, and end with a brief review of different kinds of writing you may be asked to create for a professor or boss. All the stuff in between is meant to help you craft grammatically correct and appealing sentences. Let's get started.

CHAPTER 1
Parts of Speech (Nouns, Verbs, Adjectives)

The parts of speech are like the building blocks of the English language. The simplest sentences can be a mere two words. The more you begin to understand how to build sentences, the more complex and beautiful your sentences can become. While some words convey important information such as who or what, others communicate the how. Even the tiniest words such as nor and to can share important information with the reader. But let's not get ahead of ourselves. Can you name the most basic parts of speech?

Did you name three? Five? Seven? We're going to discuss seven:

| Nouns | Verbs | Adjectives | Adverbs | Conjunctions | Prepositions | articles |

NOUNS

Nouns identify people, places or things. They may be singular and refer to a solo item, or plural, which refers to a group. There are also proper nouns, which refer to the names of specific people, places or things. Let's take a look at some examples.

People: mother, doctor, cashier, musician

Places: home, work, park, street, restaurant

Things: dog, car, tree, conversation, secret

Plural Nouns: mothers, homes, dogs

Proper Nouns: Mrs. Smith (person), Spain (place), Walmart (thing)

Now, those were the easy nouns. Next are some more advanced nouns. Nouns may also be broken down into groups according to what they describe. These groups help our brain organize the kinds of nouns we can build sentences with. Here are seven types of nouns:

Abstract These nouns describe concepts, or intangible things, that cannot be seen or touched. In other words, you can't physically collect these things—they exist as *ideas*.

- love, fear, patience, happiness, bravery

Collective These nouns describe groups of things in a single word without an "s". However, an "s" may be added when discussing multiple collective nouns. For example: The four teams completed over several days to earn the title of champion.

- team, herd, family, crowd, congregation, flock

Compound These nouns are created by putting two nouns together to refer to a single item. Compound nouns can be tricky; they can appear as a single word, as a hyphenated word, or as two separate words.

- policeman, bedroom, girlfriend, fire-fly, bathing suit, washing machine

Concrete These nouns refer to items that can be seen or touched.

- couch, flower, face, gift

Gender-specific These nouns refer to words that describe either male or female things.
- actor, actress, aunt, uncle, bull, cow

Mass These nouns refer to items that cannot be counted; they are also called non-countable nouns.

- music, heat, experience

Verbal These nouns refer to words that came from verbs; most end in the letters -ing.
- the building, the living, an arrival, a decision

Pluralizing Nouns

So what happens when you want to make a noun plural? A few different things actually; spelling can be a bit tricky. Let's review some basic spelling guidelines below when turning a singular noun into a plural one. If a word's spelling changes beyond adding an "s" at the end it's usually to aid the verbal flow of the word.

1. For the majority of nouns, simply add an "s" at the end.

a. Mother → mothers
   b. Store → stores
   c. Computer → computers

2. For most words ending in the letters -ch, -s, and –x, add an "es" to the end.

   a. Switch → switches
   b. Mass → masses
   c. Fox → foxes

3. For words ending in an "f" sound, change the f to a v and add "es".

   a. Leaf → leaves
   b. Life → lives
   c. Self → selves

4. For words ending in a consonant and the letter y, the y should change to an i before adding an "es".

   a. Baby → babies
   b. Curry → curries
   c. Flurry → flurries

5. Irregular nouns

   Some plural nouns simply don't follow the rules. For such nouns, the only option is to memorize them (or trust that your grammar program recognizes their proper form).

   a. Cactus → Cacti The cactus looked lonely in the desert. The cacti grew to form a circle.

   b. Child → children One child played on the swings. Three children played on the playground.

c. Deer → deer One deer walked through the forest. Five deer ran through field.

d. Fish → fish I caught one fish yesterday. He caught 18 fish!

e. Fungus → Fungi The fungus destroyed the tree. The fungi colony grew quickly.

f. Goose → geese The goose honked loudly. The geese flew in a V shape through the air.

g. Mouse → mice The mouse scurried quickly about the room. The mice scattered when they saw the cat.

h. Man → men The man sat on the bench. The men discussed the football game among themselves.

i. Phenomenon → Phenomena The phenomenon was a singular occurrence. The lightening phenomena became so regular it turned into a tourist attraction.

j. Person → People The person deserved the award. The people clapped during the award ceremony.

k. Woman → women The woman walked by herself. The women walked together.

Remember: exceptions to these general rules above exist. Spell Check programs will catch most errors, but they can sometimes miss mistakes, especially if a sentence uses a word differently than the program expects. It's always a good idea to double check a word's plural spelling in an online or print dictionary. It takes only mere seconds and ensures that your sentences contain properly spelled words!

VERBS

Verbs are words of action. They allow the writer or speaker to describe what the noun in is doing. The most simple sentences may contain only a noun and a verb. Let's take a look at a few simple examples:

He died.

Elizabeth laughs.

I won.

In each of the above sentences, the noun precedes the verb. Think of verbs as the Nike tagline of words (you know Nike's tagline "Just Do It"); to discover the verb in a sentence, ask yourself "What is the noun doing?", and you'll discover the action within the sentence.

Like nouns, there are several types of verbs…however they're a bit more complicated. So much so in fact that we'll be devoting a later chapter to verbs—especially those that appear in irregular forms. Most verbs adhere to a simple conjugation pattern:

Infinitive	Third Person Present	Past	Present Participle	Past Participle
Cook	Cooks	Cooked	Cooking	Cooked

- I cook a wonderful spaghetti.
- She cooks a wonderful spaghetti.
- I am cooking a wonderful spaghetti right now.
- We cooked a wonderful spaghetti yesterday.

ADJECTIVES and ADVERBS

Imagine how boring conversations would be if they were limited to merely two-word sentences:

I woke. I dressed. I ate. I drove. I arrived. I worked. She asked. I answered. I returned. I dined. I slept. I repeated.

To avoid such boredom we have adjectives and adverbs. As their name suggests, these parts of speech "add" description to a sentence. Adjectives add description to nouns and adverbs add description to verbs. These two words are often referred to as modifiers because they modify, or change, a sentence. Think of it like this: when you modify a car, you do so with the intent of improving it; you change it for the better. When you modify a sentence with adjectives and adverbs, you add more detail creating a richer, more descriptive sentence for the reader. Let's take a look at these examples.

He rolled a **red** ball. Red is an adjective. It describes the ball.

The **tall** tree swayed in the wind. Tall is an adjective. It describes the tree.

Elizabeth laughed **loudly**. Loudly is an adverb. It describes how Elizabeth laughed.

The dog ran **quickly**. Quickly is ab adverb. It describes how the dog ran.

Since adjectives describe people, places, or things, they are typically words that relate to one of the five senses; they are words that describe how someone or something looks (**pretty** flowers), tastes (**sweet** ice cream), feels (**soft** blanket), smells (**salty** air), and sounds (**soft** whisper). In English, adjectives typically come before a noun. Adverbs on the other hand describe how an action occurred: loudly, softly, quickly, slowly. Although adverbs usually appear after the verb, it is fine if they precede it.

Toby ate slowly.   OR   Toby slowly ate.   Either adverb placement is grammatically correct.

Notice a pattern? Many adverbs end in the suffix –ly. However this is not a steadfast rule; here are some adverbs that don't end in –ly.

Mike always runs in the morning. Always is an adverb. It describes how Mike runs.
I never yell. Never is an adverb. It describes how I yell.

When trying to discern if a word is an adjective, ask the noun one of these three questions: What kind of? Which one? How many? An adjective will answer these questions for you.

The happy dog dropped the new, red ball. Which dog? The **happy** one. What kind of ball? The **new, red** one.

When trying to discern if a word is an adverb, ask the verb How? When? Where? Why? How Much? How Often? To what extent?

The dancer twirled wildly across the stage. How did the dancer twirl? Wildly.

I often snore and wake myself up at night. How do I snore? Often.

CONJUNCTIONS

Conjunctions may be small words, but they're important. Think of them as the glue of the sentence building world; they join two different thoughts together cohesively. The English language has three types of conjunctions, and each has their own purpose. Let's take a look.

Coordinating Conjunctions: and, but, for, nor, or, so, yet

These conjunctions connect two ideas together. As a sentence becomes more descriptive, they can also join independent clauses, typically with a comma.

- Mark and Maria both enjoy playing hockey.

- Jose needs to drive to the grocery store, but he has a doctor's appointment first.

Subordinating Conjunctions

As their name suggests, these words subjugate, a dependent clause in a sentence. This means that the clause doesn't make sense without the rest of the sentence. There are many subordinating conjunctions; here is a short list: after, although, as, as if, as though, because, before, even though, if, once, since, than, that, though, unless, until, when, whenever, where, whereas, while.

- Becky is buying us a round of drinks since she earned a big tip tonight.

In this example, the independent clause "Becky is buying us a round of drinks" can stand by itself. The dependent clause, "since she earned a big tip tonight" must be linked to an independent clause (or complete thought), because it doesn't make sense on its own. A reader expects to learn what Becky did with the tip; therefore, it must be linked to an independent clause using a subordinating conjunction. Remember: sentences can often be arranged without losing their meaning. For example, this sentence could be rewritten with the subordinating conjunction beginning the sentence:

- Since Becky earned a big tip tonight, she's buying us a round of drinks.

Correlative Conjunctions

These conjunctions always appear in pairs. Their function in the sentence is to create equality between two ideas within the sentence. Here are six common correlative conjunction pairs:

Both…and
Either…or
Neither…nor
Not only…but also
Not…but
Whether…or

Let's take a look at an example:

"**Whether** you succeed **or** fail is irrelevant—what matters is if you tried."
In this example, the speaker gives equal importance to a person succeeding and a person failing; he draws attention to the more important idea that trying is the most important aspect of any experience.

PREPOSITIONS

Prepo- what? Prepositions are words that indicate relationships in a sentence. They usually link a noun or pronoun to something else in the sentence. Many prepositions exist in English; these words help to clarify a specific meaning in a sentence.

- I set the sword on the table.
- I set the sword in the table.
- I set the sword under the table.

In the above examples, each preposition indicates a different relationship of the sword to the table in the sentence. Though the words are small, they carry great meaning. Imagine the different meaning of each of these sentences in a scenario involving zombies; being able to communicate exactly where the sword is could be a lifesaver! Here is a list of common prepositions and their intended meaning:

To describe a single point in time: at, in, on

- The guests will arrive at 8:00 p.m.

To describe an extended time period: by, during, for, from, since, until

- During my four years at college, I hope to earn a degree in mathematics.

To describe a place: above, at, below, beneath, inside, in, on, over, under, underneath

- The dust bunnies beneath my bed are becoming dust elephants.

To describe being close to something: among, between, by, near, next to

- Between the garage and the mailbox is a beautiful flowerbed.

To describe a direction: to, into, onto

- Our family vacation to Disneyland was amazing.

You may have heard a little bit more about prepositions. It's considered bad form to end a sentence with a preposition. Although some authors may break this rule, it's a good rule to follow whether you're writing personally or professionally. It's simply more logical to establish a relationship of two things in the sentence and not at the end. We'll touch on this more in the "Avoiding Common Errors" section.

ARTICLES

Though small, articles can be mighty. These parts of speech serve an important function: they allow the speaker to convey the difference between specific and general objects. Articles are similar to adjectives in that they modify nouns. There are two types of articles: definite and indefinite.

The English language has three articles: the, a, an. The is a definite article; it always refers to a specific person, place, or thing. A and an are indefinite articles; they always refer to any person, place, or thing.

In the following examples, note how changing the article changes the meaning of the entire sentence.

"Please hand me the magazine."

"Please hand me a magazine."

In the first sentence, the phrase "the magazine" indicates the speaker has a specific magazine in mind. In the second sentence, the speaker indicates that any magazine will do; it doesn't matter which magazine he receives.

Here's the tricky part: when to use a versus when to use an. The general rule revolves around the word following the article. A and an both refer to a general, or indefinite noun. Here are the rules:

Use a if the following noun beings with a consonant: a dog, a chair, a man.

Use a if the following noun sounds like a consonant, even if it's a vowel: a university

Use a if the following noun begins with a clear H sound: a home

Use an if the following noun begins with a silent H: an hour

Use an if the following noun begins with a vowel: an eagle, an eggplant, an outbreak

If a noun is modified by an adjective, the article rules should be applied to the word immediately following the article.

- It would be difficult to find an invisible chair.

Though we would write "a chair", because invisible begins with a vowel, the correctly written phrase   becomes "an invisible chair".

- A soaring eagle is a beautiful experience to behold.

Though we would write "an eagle" and "an experience", because soaring and beautiful both begins with a consonant letter, the correctly written phrases are "a soaring eagle" and "a beautiful experience".

CHAPTER 2
Pronouns (Subject, Object, Possessive)

Now that we've covered the building blocks of sentences, let's move on to pronouns. These little words were created to alleviate reader and listener boredom. Pronouns replace nouns within a sentence. Why? Good question. Why would we ever need to replace nouns in a sentence? I'm glad you asked. Let me share the wisdom of pronouns with you.

Clara loved to be outside. Clara wanted to spend as much time outside as possible, so Clara decided to build a treehouse. After saving enough money, Clara bought lumber and supplies and Clara began building a treehouse.

That's a pretty repetitive paragraph. The reader begins to tune out after hearing about Clara so many times. Pronouns help sentences avoid repetition and maintain the reader's focus. Here's a better constructed paragraph using pronouns:

Clara loved to be outside. **She** wanted to spend as much time outside as possible, so **she** decided to build a treehouse. After saving enough money, Clara bought lumber and supplies and began building **her** treehouse.

Pronouns can be grouped into three categories: subject, object, and possessive

Subject Pronouns

Subject pronouns replace the noun completing the action (the subject) in a sentence. In English, the noun is often replaced to avoid repeating the subject within a paragraph or longer text. It is common practice to include both the original subject and the subject pronoun within a sentence and/or a paragraph. Doing so helps to maintain reader interest and engagement in a text.

Subject pronouns include the following words: I, you, he, she, it we, you, they.

Tari loves to read books. → She loves to read books.

The soccer team won the championship. → They won the championship.

The rabbit hopped quickly away from the fox. → It hopped quickly away from the fox.

I replaces a singular masculine or feminine subject.

You replaces a singular masculine or feminine subject.

He replaces a singular masculine subject.

She replaces a singular feminine subject.

It replaces a singular animal, object, or thing.

We replaces a plural masculine or feminine subject.

They replaces a plural masculine or feminine subject.

A few tips on using the pronoun it:

- It should not be used to refer to a person.

- The exception to this rule is if the noun in the sentence is a baby of unknown sex.
    - Do you know if the baby is a boy or a girl? → Do you know if it is a boy or girl?

- It is also used to discuss the weather and time.
    - The weather is rainy today → It is rainy today.
    - The time is 5:04 p.m. → It is 5:04 p.m.

Object Pronouns

While subject pronouns identify what the focus of a sentence is, objects are affected by the subject's action(s). In other words, the object receives the action. Object pronouns replace the object in a sentence to help the writer avoid repeating the same word.

Object pronouns include the following words: me, you, him, her, it, us, them.

Did you call me?
Students really respect him.

Dogs love her.
Where did you leave it?

Possessive Pronouns

This group of pronouns is used to indicate ownership in a sentence. These pronouns can refer to singular or plural ownership. This means that an object can be owned by a single individual or by a group of people.

Possessive pronouns include the following words: my, mine, your, yours, his, her, hers, its, our, ours, their, theirs, whose.

Possessive pronouns are best understood in context, so here it goes.

My dog will win the Frisbee championship.   (Sounds better than The dog I own..)

"That phone is mine!"

Your cat just bit me.

Yours is a truly awful car.

His act of kindness will change thousands of lives.

Her attitude needs some adjustment.

"Is this pen hers?"

The dog wagged its tail.

Our new home is beautiful.

That basketball is ours.

Their next game will determine the championship match

Is theirs the last house on the right?

Whose book is this?

CHAPTER 3
Verbs and Their Tenses (Present + Past + Future)

Now that you know verbs are words of action, it's time to explore when that action is taking place. Verbs can change their form, or how they appear, so writers and speakers can clearly share *when* events took place. In other words, verbs tell the reader if a certain action is occurring in the past, present, or future.

Here's the tricky part: within the past, present, and future verb tenses, each can be further broken down according to the writer or speaker's intention. For example, there is a big difference between the following sentences:

Matt went to the doctor's office.

Matt was going to go to the doctor's office.

Both of these events happened in the past. However, in the first sentence the action is certain: Matt went to the doctor's office. However, in the second sentence although Matt intended to go, he didn't. This leads the reader to wonder what interrupted Matt, and if he ever got to the doctor's office. The verb tense writers use conveys a great deal of information in the sentence. Here are the many verb tenses in English and what each is used to convey in a sentence.

So how many verb tenses are there total? Twelve. Yup. There are twelve different ways to identify exactly when an action took place. Here's how the three main tenses may be further broken down:

- The Present Tense
    - Present Continuous
    - Present Perfect
    - Present Perfect Continuous

- The Past Tense
    - Past Continuous
    - Past Perfect
    - Past Perfect Continuous

- The Future Tense
    - Future Continuous
    - Future Perfect

- Future Perfect Continuous

Are all of these delineations really necessary? Yup. That's the short answer. Read on to discover the small, yet important differences between the verb tenses.

The Present Tense

We use this tense to describe a general action. The action may occur a single time or it may happen repeatedly. It may also be referred to as the simple present tense. Writers often use this tense to characterize the characters within their novel.

- I read books.
- He walks dogs.
- We did not clean today.

The present tense speaks generally about the present:

Question: "What do you do?"

Answer: "I write song lyrics."

It's important to remember that while an added –s at the end of a noun signifies a change of quantity (a book = 1 book while the books refers to a group), adding an –s at the end of the verb does not signify that the action was done repeatedly or longer. Adding an –s at the end of a verb simply conjugates the verb to reflect the third person (he, she, it) subject.

The Present Continuous

This tense describes a particular event occurring immediately. However, it may also be used to describe an event that will occur in the close future if a context word appears in the sentence. The present continuous requires an auxiliary verb in order to work.

- I am reading books.
- He is walking dogs next week.

- We are not going to cook today.

While the present tense suggests an action that is happening currently, it does not necessarily pinpoint when it is occurring. The present continuous tense exists to identify what is happening right now:

Question: "What are you doing?"

Answer: "I am writing a book!"

The Present Perfect

This tense acts as a bridge between the past and the present. Writers use this tense to describe experiences to their audience; it can also be used to show a situational change or continuing situation. It always requires the helping verb "have".

- I have enjoyed our conversations.

- Susan has completed her doctoral degree.

- They have never volunteered their time to a charitable organization.

This tense implies that although an action is currently happening in the present, it has also happened in the past (or never happened at all). The present perfect tense is wonderful in creating resumes as the writer can highlight skills developed over a period of time.

Question: "What skills will you bring to this new position?"

Answer: "I have worked at my current job for 11 years. During this time, I have developed many processes that increased efficiency and decreased waste."

The Present Perfect Continuous

I know, it's a tongue-twister of a name. This tense does everything that the present perfect tense does but it communicates that the ongoing action will be stopping in the present. It may be stopping immediately, or in the near present. To do this, the present perfect continuous tense needs two auxiliary verbs: have and been.

- My father, who has been working for forty-two years, will retire next month.

- We have been listening to this boring lecture for nearly two hours!

This tense typically conveys how an individual, group, or program has been spending its time; it provides important details that help to characterize the subject of the sentence.

Question: Why did you decide to change careers?

Answer: Well, I had been working in banking for twelve years when I decided I needed a change; running an organic farm has been a dream of mine since I could remember.

The Past

Also called the simple past, this tense shares that an action has occurred in the past. Now, this action may have happened in the recent past or 3,000 years ago. However, there is no question that the action happened; the simple past verb tense indicates the certainty of an action. Unlike other past verb tenses, the simple past tense does not influence the present. Regular verb forms will end in –ed. If a sentence is constructed negatively, then it will require an auxiliary verb.

- Tom lived in Canada.

- Mary bought a house.

- Tom did not live in Mexico.

Although most verbs simply add an –ed (baked, walked, jumped, barked) at the end to create the simple past tense, some pesky irregular verbs exist. No trick exists to know if a verb is irregular; unfortunately, you simply need to learn and remember them. The good news is that the more you read and listen to conversations, the more likely you'll be to recognize them and use them correctly when writing and speaking. Print and online dictionaries are both excellent resources. Curious about irregular verbs? Here are a few.

| Sing | Sung |
| Bend | Bent |

Bite	Bit
Buy	Bought
Choose	Chose
Dive	Dove
Write	Wrote
Eat	Ate
Feel	Felt
Dig	Dug
Think	Thought
Speak	Spoke

The Past Continuous

This tense is a favorite among both mystery and memoir writers. The past continuous tense allows a writer to pinpoint a specific time in the past. Well-written sentences using this tense almost always provide context clues to the specific moment in the past. The past continuous requires "be" as its auxiliary verb. But remember, "be" is the most irregular verb of them all! Here are all the verb forms of "to be": am, are, is, was, were, been, being.

- "Judge, it wasn't me. I was fishing with my brother when my wife disappeared."

- Once, when I was climbing a huge oak, I fell and broke my arm. That was the moment I knew I wanted to become a doctor.

This verb tense is great for recalling memories of a specific moment instead of a general past event.

Question: "What is your favorite memory?"

Answer: "When I was five, I was building a snowman and saw this dog walking down the road. We took him in and he was the best dog we ever rescued."

The Past Perfect

Because life is a series of events, sometimes we need to highlight the order of these events so that they make sense. The past perfect tense shares an event that happened before another event in the past. This allows the writer to describe two events occurring in the past in relationship to one another. This tense is important, especially in narrative writing to properly sequence events. The past perfect requires had as an auxiliary verb.

- The coach yelled at her after she had dismounted.

- Amaya skipped down the hallway; she had passed all of her semester exams.

Each of these sentences orders two past events for the reader. In the first sentence, a coach waited to yell at an athlete; so the athlete got off a piece of equipment and then listened to the coach yell. In the second sentence, Amaya first took the exams and then skipped down the hallway after discovering she had passed every one.

Question: Can you recall the events of September 5th?

Answer: Well, I opened my door and immediately noticed someone had ransacked the living room.

The Past Perfect Continuous

This tense describes an action that occurred over a period of time in the past. It may describe an event that lasted an hour or an event that transpired over days, weeks, or years. The past perfect continuous needs two auxiliary verbs: had and been.

- The storm had been raging for hours before the sun finally peeked through the clouds.

- The farmers had been hoping for rain for months.

Context clues can help a reader understand the implied length of the action occurring in the past. In the above examples, the context clues of hours and months help the reader understand the relationship of the subjects to the action in the sentences.

Question: "What's the best piece of advice you have for others?"

Answer: "Well, up until a certain point, I had been listening to everybody else. Then I just started listening to myself. And that's when everything just fell into place."

The Future

This tense shares that an action will occur in the future. The action can occur tomorrow or in 3,000 years. Predictions are often made with the simple future tense. Negative sentence constructions require an auxiliary verb.

The simple future tense inserts the word "will" in front of a present tense verb. The word "will" strongly indicates that an action will occur in the future. Ultimately, the simple future conveys that an action hasn't happened yet but that the action is very likely to occur sometime in the future.

- Tom will live in Canada.

- Mary thinks she will buy a home.

- Tom will not live in Mexico.

When reading or writing the simple future, it's important to remember that many people use contractions with this verb tense. For example, the sentence "I'll walk on Mars" is actually "I will walk on Mars". It's also common practice to use the verb think with the future tense; the verb think reinforces that the main action hasn't happened yet, but is likely to happen in the future.

Question: Do you have any plans tomorrow?

Answer: I think I'll (I will) exercise then head to the park.

The Future Continuous

Like the past continuous, the future continuous allows the writer to identify a specific moment—but in the future. A well-written sentence will also identify the moment that the action will be taking place. To create this tense, a writer needs to use will and be as auxiliary verbs.

- Sally will be driving across the country this summer.

- We will be travelling to Italy to celebrate Nona's 85th birthday in two years.

This tense is a favorite among weather forecasters; after all, they're always describing a future event for their viewers:

Question: What will the weather be like tomorrow?

Answer: Tomorrow, the weather will be raining in the morning, but sunny by 3 p.m.

The Future Perfect

We use this tense to share an action that will be done in the future; it is most often used to describe an intended goal. In essence, this tense conveys the past in the future. The future perfect tense needs the helping verbs will and have.

- Our company will have decided upon the best candidate for the position by Monday.

- The rescue dog will have trained for two years before going out on a solo mission.

In both of these examples, the speaker describes how an event will be finished at a stated date in the future. In the first example, although the company has not yet decided upon a candidate, they will have a decision on a specific date in the future. In the second example, although the dog has not yet finished its training, the training will be complete after two years.

Question: When will you earn your doctorate degree?

Answer: I will have earned my doctorate degree after four years of study, an internship, and a thesis dissertation.

The Future Perfect Continuous

While the future perfect allows the speaker to convey a specific event ending in the future, the future perfect continuous tense allows the speaker to convey that an ongoing event will end at a point in the future. This tense is most often used to describe an action that a person has been doing over a long period of time. To create this tense, three auxiliary verbs must be used: will, have, been.

- Melissa, a championship dancer, will have been competing for fifteen years this June.

- Our librarian will have been organizing story time for twenty-two years this summer.

This tense is often used when providing background about an individual or program in both fiction and non-fiction. It allows a writer to share traits or experiences that have occurred over a long period of time.

Question: How long have you been mentoring students after school?

Answer: I will have been mentoring students for fifteen years this coming September.

To select the proper verb tense, a writer must first determine if the action is occurring in the present, has already occurred in the past, or will be occurring in the future. Once this has been determined, a writer can further narrow down the action and craft the sentence accordingly.

CHAPTER 4
A Note on Irregular Verbs

While most verbs in the English language follow a typical pattern, some do not. Though this is not a complete list, it's a pretty good start. Unfortunately, there is no pattern to irregular verbs; their simple past and past participle forms just need to be memorized.

Infinitive	Simple Past	Past Participle
Be	Was, were	Been
Begin	Began	Begun
Bite	Bit	bitten
Break	Broke	broken
Choose	Chose	Chosen
Do	Did	done
Draw	Drew	Drawn
Drink	Drank	drunk
Eat	Ate	eaten
Fly	Flew	Flown
Forgive	Forgave	Forgiven
Give	Gave	Given
Grow	Grew	Grown
Know	Knew	Known
Outdo	Outdid	Outdone
Redo	Redid	Redone
Ring	Rang	Rung
Rise	Rose	Risen
Shake	Shook	Shaken
Sing	Sang	Sung
Speak	Spoke	Spoken
Swim	Swam	Swum
Take	Took	Taken
Wear	Wore	Worn
Write	Wrote	Written

Here are some examples of irregular verbs in sentences:

The priest rose early each morning to **ring** the churches bells; after the last bell had **rung**, he descended the steps to begin his daily prayers.

As a young girl the artist would **draw** every day; over her lifetime she **drew** more than 500 portraits. Each one was **drawn** with the same haunting eyes.

The child couldn't wait to **grow** up and be tall like his father. His mother measured him every month to see if he had **grown**. He was certain that he **grew** every night while he slept!

"Hey! Do you want to **swim** in the lake?"

"No thanks. I **swam** there yesterday. I'm heading to the pool today."

CHAPTER 5
Punctuation and Style (Do Not Miss Out On This!)

Punctuation can be just as important as the words within a sentence. Incorrectly punctuating a sentence can actually dramatically change the meaning of a sentence. Lynne Truss, author of *Eats, Shoots & Leaves* created a famous example of just how important punctuation can be in creating sentence meaning for a reader. Take a look at her example:

The panda eats shoots and leaves.

The panda eats, shoots, and leaves.

In the first sentence, the panda is enjoying a plant-based meal.

In the second sentence, the panda enjoys three separate actions: eating, shooting, and leaving. This sentence causes the reader to wonder what the panda ate and what the panda shot. Of course, the reader is also left wonder how the panda got a gun in the first place.

This of course is a clever example. However it does demonstrate how punctuation can dramatically change the meaning of a sentence. All punctuation marks have an important purpose; some actually have several different important purposes. Whether you need to end an idea or communicate extreme emotion such as fear or joy, punctuation is there to help you achieve these goals (and many more!).

So how many punctuation marks do you need to intimately know? Just about fourteen. Can you correctly name each of the following?

.	
,	
:	
;	
'	
" "	
( )	
[ ]	
/	
-	
—	

!	
?	
...	

How many did you correctly name? Let's find out:

.	Period
,	Comma
:	Colon
;	Semi-colon
'	Apostrophe
" "	Quotation Marks
( )	Parentheses
[ ]	Brackets
/	Slash Mark
-	Hyphen
—	Dash
!	Exclamation Mark
?	Question Mark
...	Ellipses

Whew! That's a lot to remember. So why bother learning the differences between all these punctuation marks? Because it's important. There's a big difference between the following phrases:

I said, "No."
I said, "No!"
I said, "No—"
I said, "No?"
I said, "No…"

Although the words above are exactly the same, the meaning changes with each punctuation mark. Some of the statements above convey strong emotions such as the period and exclamation point where others convey an unfolding situation such as the dash and ellipses, which indicate an interruption and trailing off respectively.

While some punctuation may have a single job, such as the exclamation point, other marks can wear multiple hats. Let's review punctuation and how it can be used to create good sentences.

The Period .

Think of the period as the stop sign of punctuation. When a period appears in a sentence it means that the thought is over, and a new thought will begin in the next sentence.

- Tomorrow is my birthday. I hope that all my friends will be able to make the party.

Although the period's main function is to indicate the complete stop of a thought, it may also be used to separate numbers when writing to indicate the correct amount in written form.

- The shirt is $9.50 on sale.

The period plays an important role in writing numbers; there is a big difference between $950 and $9.50!

Dates can sometimes be written with periods as well. When written this way, periods separate the month, day, and year for the reader. It's important to remember that different cultures write dates differently.   Typically English speakers arrange dates by month then day then year.

- September 2, 2015   →   09.02.2015

Finally, periods are also used when abbreviating a word. If the abbreviated word ends a sentence, then an additional period is not necessary.

- My alarm clock buzzed at 6:10 a.m.

- Eliza's new address is 101 Dorsey Rd., Cooksville, AL 12345.

Here are a few common abbreviations, and what they stand for:

Acad.	Academy
A.D.	Anno Domini (in the year of the Lord)
Ave.	Ante meridiem (before noon)
Ave.	Avenue
B.A.	Bachelor of Arts (academic degree)
B.C.	Before Christ
B.S.	Bachelor of Science (academic degree)
Capt.	Captain

Corp.	Corporation
Dr.	Doctor
Et al.	Et alii (and others)
Jr.	Junior
Sr.	Senior
Mr.	Mister
Mrs.	Mistress (refers to a married woman)
Ms.	Miss (refers to a young or unmarried woman)
Vs.	Versus

The Comma ,

It's a common misperception that commas indicate pauses in a sentence. Though this may be true some of the time, it is not true most of the time. The main function of commas is twofold. First, and easiest to remember: commas separate items in a list. This helps to avoid confusion when reading lists (remember the gun-happy panda bear?). Second, commas connect dependent clauses to independent clauses. Huh? A dependent clause isn't a sentence on its own. An independent clause can stand alone as a sentence. We'll get to these in a moment, but first items in a list.

- Please pick up a green, tomatoes, and carrots at the store.

Now about clauses. Here's an independent clause: Sinead became a model. This is a short, yet complete thought. But most times, we want to know more information…so we may add a dependent clause such as this: Sinead became a model, and she traveled all over the world. The added phrase after the comma "and she traveled all over the world" is a dependent clause—it doesn't make sense if read on its own. Writers can join the two phrases together with a comma to create one detailed sentence for the reader.

Commas also follow introductory phrases. These phrases are dependent on the independent phrase that follows them. For example: Tall and striking, no one questioned Sinead's choice to become a model. The phrase "tall and striking" introduces characteristics about the subject, Sinead.

Likewise, commas follow introductory clauses. While an introductory phrase lacks a subject, an introductory clause contains a subject and a verb. For example: Because Sinead was tall and striking, she became a model.

Commas usually follow phrases or clauses beginning with the following introductory words:
also, alternatively, although, always, because, furthermore, however, in order to, never, similarly, since, therefore, though, thus

Introductory elements help writers establish the relationship between sentences. For example, the word furthermore indicates that the next idea will strengthen an already established argument whereas the world although indicates the writer is making a concession and acknowledging a contrary piece of information.

Now onto everything else comma! Here are six comma rules that will improve your sentence-writing abilities!

1. Use commas after every three digits beyond 999.
    a. 1,000   10,000   100,000   1,000,000

2. Use commas to separate months and dates from years.
    a. My birthday is March 3, 1980.

3. Use commas to separate cities from states in an address.
    a. Travis Whitmore
       123 Flagmore St.
       Covington, ME 12345

4. Use commas to separate cities from countries in sentences.
    a. Paris, France is rich with history and artwork.

5. Use commas to surround a person being addressed in a sentence.
    a. Hello, Samda, it's nice to see you!

6. Use commas to surround a person's title or degree that follows their name.
    a. Dr. Camut, PhD, will be taking students to Australia this semester.

The Colon :

This punctuation mark is used to create emphasis. A writer can use a colon within a sentence three ways: to introduce a list, to restate an idea, or to introduce a long quotation. Think of it this way: what follows a colon is important. Colons are also used following a business salutation.

1. Colons introduce items in a list after an independent clause
    a. During the winter Olympics we watched many events: ice skating, hockey, luge, and skiing.

2. Colons introduce a restated idea to stress its importance.
    a. Marriage vows are sacred: they cement the commitment two people pledge to each other forever.

3. Colons introduce long quotations in a text (5 or more lines).
    a. In Shakespeare's *Hamlet*, the main character gives the best speech in the play:

    > To be, or not to be: that is the question:
    >   Whether 'tis nobler in the mind to suffer
    >   The slings and arrows of outrageous fortune,
    >   Or to take arms against a sea of troubles,
    >   And by opposing end them? To die: to sleep;
    >   No more; and by a sleep to say we end
    >   The heart-ache and the thousand natural shocks…

4. Colons should follow business salutations.
    a. Dear Director Cahill:
    b. To Whom it May Concern:

The Semicolon ;

This punctuation marks appears as a period above a comma—and for good reason. A semicolon's main function is to connect two independent clauses. So why wouldn't you just use a period? Great question. A semicolon connects two closely related sentences. The second sentence may directly illuminate the first, or it may provide contrast to encourage the reader to think about the presented differences. At any rate, semicolons help to increase the idea flow within the paragraph. If the period is a stop sign, the semicolon is a yield sign. Here are the rules:

1. Semicolons connect two (or more) independent clauses.

    a. I am committed to a weekly workout routine; I go to the gym three times a week, lift weights twice a week, and swim at the pool on the weekends.

2. Semicolons precede conjunctive adverbs in a sentence.

    a. Doctors make pretty good money; therefore, many college students choose medicine as their future career.

    b. Common conjunctive adverbs: accordingly, also, certainly, consequently, furthermore, however, incidentally, indeed, moreover, nevertheless, otherwise, therefore, thus, undoubtedly

3. Semicolons introduce a contrast of ideas.

    a. I think Brad Pitt will win the Oscar; however, my sister thinks Johnny Depp will win.

4. Semicolons separate a list within a list.

    a. I have visited many places including Ottawa, Canada; Moscow, Russia; Dublin, Ireland; and Tokyo, Japan.

The Apostrophe '

Think of this punctuation mark as an upside down comma in the air. The apostrophe has three main purposes in the English language: to indicate possession, to create a contraction, and to alert the reader to missing letters. Here's what you need to know:

1. Apostrophes can form singular or plural possession.

    a. Singular: The boy's book fell off the table.
        i. The book belongs to the boy. For singular possession, the apostrophe precedes the s.

    b. Plural: The boys' toys littered the floor.
        i. The toys belong to a group of boys. For plural possession, the apostrophe follows the s.

2. Apostrophes help to create contractions. Contractions evolved as our speech evolved; apostrophes indicate where letters have been omitted.

    a. I will → I'll
    b. He is → he's

c. Would not → wouldn't

3. Apostrophes indicate missing letters. People often drop letters when speaking; writers often use apostrophes when capturing dialogue.

    a. 'cause   I'm going to the park **'cause** I need some quiet time to think. (because)

    b. Sayin'   Mark's just **sayin'** that he's sorry. He didn't mean to hurt your feelings. (saying)

Quotation Marks "   "   and '   '

Quotation marks always appear in pairs. There are two types of quotation marks: single and double. The rules are straightforward for quotation marks.

1. Double quotation marks surround primary source material and dialogue.

    a. A primary source is any source you directly quote from the original text. Dialogue is anything people say.
    b. Primary Source: In Shakespeare's *Hamlet*, the bard philosophically writes "There is nothing either good or bad, but thinking makes it so."
    c. Dialogue: "Good afternoon, sir. Do you have a reservation?"
        "I do. It should be under Rockefeller."

2. Single quotation marks surround secondary source material (a quotation within a quotation).

    a. If while conducting research a book quotes another book, and you want to quote the quotation, single quotation marks should be used to indicate you are citing information another source has already cited.

So what's with the two different types of quotation marks? Well, source material is an important thing; people like to know that the information they're learning about is reliable. Primary source material is the strongest material when gathering information because it hasn't been diluted; no words have been changed or meaning slightly rearranged to fit another's purpose. Single quotation marks alert the reader that the information is at least two sources removed and may not be as reliable.

Parentheses ( )

The parentheses punctuation mark always appears in a pair. This is because the function of the parentheses is to surround supplemental details—these are details that provide new but not crucial information to the reader. They always appear in pairs to mark the beginning and the end of the additional details.

- Hiking (the best kind of outdoor exercise) is a wonderful way to reconnect with nature.

Parentheses are also used when citing information in an academic paper. The type of information included inside the parentheses depends upon the method of citation. For rules on how to properly cite research for a paper, consult the proper formatting guide. Different disciplines use different citation (and therefore different parentheses methods).

Occasionally, this punctuation mark is also used to include important dates of interest within a sentence.   In the following example, including the birth date for Neil Armstrong provides a historical reference point for readers who may be unfamiliar with this man and/or historical event.

- Neil Armstrong (b. 1930) was the first person to walk on the moon.

Finally, parentheses can be used to indicate that a noun may be plural. This is often used to express uncertainty.

- The senior(s) behind this prank may rest assured that detention will follow.

Brackets [ ]

Like parentheses, brackets always appear in pairs. They also contain additional information. However, this punctuation mark should be used sparingly when writing.

1. Use brackets to add clarifying details to quotations.

    a. "Bruce Springsteen [a famous musician] is known for his lyrics focusing on blue-collar America and political activism."

2. Use brackets to modify a quotation by adding emphasis through italics, underlining, or bolding.

    a. "By the year 2050 a *significant* number of the world's food crops may be extinct due to climate change [emphasis added]."

3. Use brackets to identify a mistake within quoted material with the insertion [sic].

    a. "According to a recent poll, 45% of college students believe that there [sic] student loans will lead to crippling debt."

    b. In the above sentence, there is incorrect; the correct word is their.

The Slash /

The slash punctuation mark is used to separate two items. It can separate numbers, letters, or words. Its purpose is to create clarity within a sentence.

1. Use a slash mark when writing fractions.

    a. The recipe calls for ½ cup of sugar.

    b. However, if a sentence begins with a fraction, spell it out using a hyphen.

        i. One-half of the global workforce does not earn a living wage.

2. Use a slash mark when writing dates.

    a. Many lives were lost on 9/11.

3. Use a slash mark to provide options in a sentence.

    a. Julio couldn't decide if he wanted fruit and/or a bagel for breakfast.

4. Use a slash mark to indicate when a line of poetry ends in a quotation.

    a. Shakespeare's *Romeo and Juliet* contains the most romantic lines describing love: "My bounty is as boundless as the sea,/My love as deep; the more I give to thee,/The more I have, for both are infinite."

Hyphen -

The hyphen can serve several purposes in a sentence. First, it helps to create compound words. Second, it helps to create written numbers to avoid confusion. Third, it helps writers write prefixes. Here are some examples.

1. Use hyphens to combine two words, typically adjectives that describe a noun.

    a. The red-haired child won the potato sack race in under two minutes.

2. Use hyphens to write numbers from twenty-one to ninety-nine.

    a. The firefighters rescued twenty-eight people from the apartment building.

3. Use hyphens to write fractions.

    a. Two-thirds of the graduating class plan to pursue a college degree.

4. Use hyphens to add a prefix before a proper noun.

    a. The ex-President plans to attend the next Nobel Prize ceremony.

5. Use hyphens to separate prefixes from root words if the prefix ends with and the root word begins with the same vowel.

    a. No one could re-enter the building once the alarm went off.

6. Use hyphens to separate a prefix from a root word to eliminate confusion if the word takes on a different meaning.

    a. Re-cover and recover

    b. Re-cover means to put a cover on something again whereas recover means to get better.

      i. Marlene re-covered the food at the picnic to keep bugs away.

      ii. My dog finally recovered from surgery after two months.

Exclamation Points !

While some punctuation marks may have many different purposes, the exclamation mark has a singular focus: to show emotion. Now, this emotion may be positive as in surprise or joy, or it may be negative as in fear or anger. The stronger the emotion, the more appropriate it is to use an exclamation mark.

1. Use an exclamation mark to show strong emotion.

    a. "Christmas is the best holiday EVER!" Christina yelled as she excitedly unwrapped gifts.

2. Use an exclamation mark following an interjection.

    a. Wow! I didn't know that butterflies could fly that far.

    b. Hey! Didn't I meet you at the holiday party?

Although it may be tempting to use many exclamation marks to show extreme emotion, it is customary to use a single exclamation mark. Should you choose to use more than one, be cautious with the additional exclamation marks. This punctuation mark is effective because it is sparingly used. Overuse simply looks cluttered on the page and makes the idea seem hokey rather than important:

- I said, "No!"

- I said, "No!!!"

The second example just seems to be overkill, doesn't it?

The Question Mark ?

The question mark exists to fulfill a single purpose: to signal uncertainty. This punctuation mark always appears at the end of a sentence. While a period communicates the end of a thought, and an exclamation point conveys strong emotion, the question mark signifies an uncertainty. A question mark communicates that the speaker is seeking an answer, or encouraging the reader to consider a rhetorical question.

1. Use a question mark when seeking an answer.
    a. What is the largest planet in our solar system?
    b. Who do you think will win the next presidential election?
    c. Would you ever lie?

2. Use a question mark when asking a rhetorical question.
    a. Are you serious?
    b. Is the Pope Catholic?

CHAPTER 6
Types of Sentences (Simple, Compound, Complex!)

Now that you've got the building blocks of sentences down, let's move onto the three main types of sentences: simple, compound, and complex. Though you may be tempted to label an extremely long sentence as complex, that's not the way it works. A simple sentence can be longer than a complex sentence. The key is to determine *how* the sentence is constructed.

Simple Sentences

Simple sentences are also called independent clauses. These sentences are the most basic; they contain a subject and a verb. However, the subject and verb are often modified to provide more detail to the reader. They should convey one clear idea. The first sentence below is an example of a very basic simple sentence. The second example contains modifiers.

1. The owl flew.
2. The owl flew gracefully between the trees.

Simple sentences may contain a compound noun and/or a compound verb. This means that there may be two nouns and/or two verbs in a single sentence.

1. The owl and bat flew between the trees gracefully.
2. The owl flew and swooped between the trees gracefully.
3. The owl and bat flew and swooped between the trees gracefully.

Compound Sentence

A compound sentence takes a simple sentence and adds on another simple sentence. The two sentences can be joined by one of three ways. First, they can be combined by a coordinating conjunction: for, and, nor, but, or, yet, so. A common acronym to help remember these little words is FANBOYS. Compound sentences allow the writer to present the reader with two ideas that are linked.

- Kristen went to the farmers' market, but none of the farmers had peaches today.

In this example, the two independent clauses are linked with the conjunction "but". It makes sense to link these two ideas because the second implies why she went to the farmers' market; it continues the idea presented in the first independent clause.

Compound sentences can also be joined by a semicolon: Kristen went to the farmers' market; it was the favorite part of her Saturday morning.

Finally, two independent clauses can be joined with a comma but only if the clauses are being used as an item in a series: Kristen bought carrots, Emma bought radishes, and Celeste bought blueberries.

Complex Sentence

Complex sentences are created by combining an independent clause with one or more dependent clauses. Dependent clauses describe the independent clause but are lacking a subject or verb; they cannot stand on their own as a sentence. One independent clause can be surrounded by several dependent clauses. Complex sentences often contain a subordinator such as although, after, because, since, or when (this is not a complete list).

- Although Elaine loves to dance, her husband prefers a good movie.

Remember: the length of a sentence doesn't determine the type of sentence. Take a look at the following sentences:

- Because I spent all week studying, I aced my English exam. (Complex)

- My favorite restaurant prepares the absolutely best gazpacho soup with produce and herbs grown hydroponically throughout the restaurant. (Simple)

CHAPTER 7
Building a Strong Sentence, The Right Way!

This is a short but important chapter. As you know, the shortest complete sentences are two words. (You may often see single words appearing as a sentence, especially in dialogue, and this is fine). However, whether you're writing creatively or academically, personally or professionally, you should strive to create longer sentences which provide specific, important details to the reader. The longer your sentences become the more they need punctuation to communicate effectively. Though you needn't surpass James Joyce's famous 4,391 word sentence, sentences with some meat are always preferable. Let's take a look at how to build a sentence.

Begin with a subject and a verb.

He sat.

Add some modifiers (adjectives and adverbs) to describe the subject and the verb.

The old man sat quietly.

Add some context to the sentence with phrases.

The old man sat quietly on the park bench feeding the pigeons.

Connect this independent clause to a dependent clause.

The old man sat quietly on the park bench feeding the pigeons, thinking of his family.

Add modifiers to the dependent clause to add detail.

The old man sat quietly on the park bench feeding the pigeons, fondly thinking of his family.

Connect this sentence to another independent clause.

The old man sat quietly on the park bench feeding the pigeons, fondly thinking of his family; he
wondered if they thought of him as frequently as he thought of them.

Add any clarifying details to create a more vivid sentence.

On a crisp autumn afternoon, the old man sat quietly on the faded park bench feeding the pigeons, fondly thinking of his family; he wondered if his five children thought of him as frequently as he thought of them.

The great thing about punctuation is that it allows you as the writer to continually add details to a sentence to create a vivid picture for your audience. Once you have the core part of a sentence, the subject and the action, you can build whatever sentence you desire. Don't be afraid to edit and revise your sentences.

When building sentences, it's important to keep the purpose of your writing in mind. While long, descriptive sentences are appropriate for narrative works, short, crisp sentences are more appropriate in a professional setting, especially when writing reports or emails.

CHAPTER 8
Avoiding Common Errors (Capitalization, Homophones, Etc)

The errors discussed in this chapter occur often due to lack of knowledge or simple laziness. Sometimes they happen because Spell Check programs aren't exactly sure of the writer's intention. Whatever the reason, the best way to avoid them is to simply know the rules. Here they are:

Capitalization

Knowing what to capitalize can be difficult. The first words of sentences are always capitalized to acknowledge the beginning of a new idea. Generally, specific words or phrases are capitalized out of a sign of respect; this is why we capitalize proper nouns. Here's what you need to know:

1. Capitalize the titles of people and publications.
    a. General Smith will be taking over the command.
    b. *The Wall Street Journal* is an excellent source for business news.

2. Capitalize proper nouns (the names of people, places, or things including religious deities or special artifacts).
    a. My family is visiting Yellowstone National Park this summer.
    b. Did you hear that Brad Pitt is directing a new movie?
    c. Do you prefer to shop at Target or Walmart?
    d. Across the world, many people believe in a higher power including Allah, Buddha, and God.

3. Capitalize historic events.
    a. The ramifications of the Vietnam War are still evident today.

4. Capitalize languages, nationalities, and races.
    a. Penny can speak several languages including Spanish and Italian.
    b. My heritage is Irish, Dutch, and Native American.

5. Capitalize the words federal and state if they are part of a title.
    a. The California State Constitution is undergoing some revisions.

6. Capitalize days, months, and holidays.
    a. This year Christmas will take place on the fourth Tuesday in December.

Dangling Modifiers

A dangling what? Modifier. A dangling modifier is a word or phrase that lacks a subject. In essence, it's a descriptive word or phrase with nothing nearby to describe. This common error creates confusion for the reader because he or she is unsure what the word or phrase is describing in the sentence.

- With a triumphant smile, the wedding dress was bought.

In the above example, it sounds as though the wedding dress is smiling…and that can't be correct. The "triumphant smile" actually refers to an absent subject, which is why this phrase is a dangling modifier…it's just dangling in the sentence! To correct a dangling modifier, simply add the subject—the "what" or "who" in the sentence.

- With a triumphant smile, the bride bought the wedding dress.
- With a triumphant smile, Sue bought the wedding dress.

Ending Sentences with Prepositions

Here is the rule: don't do it. Since prepositions are words that indicate a relationship between two things, it's important to establish the relationship instead of leaving it hanging at the end of the sentence. To correct a sentence ending with a preposition, you'll need to rewrite some or a big chunk of it. Furthermore, sentences ending with prepositions can be clunky and can nearly always be rewritten to sound better.

- Incorrect: I sat watching a butterfly as it flew right by.

- Correct: I watched a butterfly fly right by me.

- Incorrect: My dog and his leash got tangled because he was running around.

- Correct: My dog's leash became tangled when he ran around a tree.

- Because my dog was running around, his leash became quite tangled.

When a sentence ends in a preposition, the relationship between two ideas may not be clear. For example in the first sentence, the reader wonders what the butterfly flew by: it could be the speaker, a flower, or spaceship. In the second example, the reader wonders how the leash became tangled. Either of the revised sentences adds clarity and helps to avoid confusion.

Homophones

Homophones are words that sound the same but have different meanings. These words may be spelled identically but have different meanings, or be spelled differently and have different meanings. Wondering why English is so confusing? It's due to its many influences from other languages. Here are some common homophones:

Ad	Ad is short for advertisement	add	Add means to count together.
Ant	Ant is an insect	Aunt	Aunt refers to your mother's sister.
Ate	Ate is the past tense of eat.	Eight	Eight refers to a number.
Bear	Bear is an animal. It also refers to carrying weight.	Bare	Bare means to reveal.
Buy	Buy is a verb meaning to purchase.	Bye	Bye is an acknowledgement that someone is leaving.
Cell	Cell refers to a biological entity.	Sell	Sell refers to the act of taking payment for something.
Die	Die refers to the cessation of life.	Dye	Dye refers to changing the color of something.
Flare	Flare refers to a small explosion to signal something.	Flair	Flair refers to being dramatic or captivating.
Knew	Knew is the past tense of know.	New	New refers to something that didn't exist before.
Hair	Hair is a body part.	Hare	Hare is a type of rabbit.
Hoard	Hoard means to gather many things.	Horde	Horde refers to a large group of people.
Hole	Hole refers to a piece that is missing.	Whole	Whole refers to something that is complete.
I	I is a pronoun referring to a person.	Eye	Eye is a body part responsible for sight.
Know	Know refers to having knowledge about something.	No	No is the opposite of yes.
Knight	Knight is a type of solider.	Night	Night is the opposite of day.

Pear	Pear is a type of fruit.	Pair	Pair refers to two of something.
Wait	Wait is a verb referring to inaction.	Weight	Weight refers to something's heaviness.
Through	Through means into or out of.	Threw	Threw is the past tense of throw.
You	You is a pronoun.	Ewe	Ewe is a female sheep.
Your	Your is a possessive pronoun indicating ownership.	You're	You're is a contraction of the words you and are.
Its	Its is a possessive pronoun indicating ownership.	It's	It's is a contraction of the words it and is
Site	Site refers to a place.	Sight	Sight refers to vision.
Too	Too means additionally or excessively	Two	Two is a number.
There	There refers to a place	Their	There is a possessive pronoun indicating ownership
They're	They're is a contraction of the words they and are.		

Commonly Confused Words

Although the following words do not sound identical, they both appear and sound very similar. So similar in fact, they are often misused. Such words may not be detected by a computer program so you need to simply be aware of the correct context for each word. Here are the fifteen most misused word pairs and how you should use them correctly in a sentence. For a more comprehensive list, simply conduct a web search for "commonly confused words".

1. Accept and Except
   Accept means to receive: He accepted my apology.

   Except: means to leave out: Shelia took all the cookies except one.

2. Affect and Effect

   Affect is typically a verb meaning to influence: The storm affected the family's travel plans.

   Effect is typically a noun meaning a result: The effect of global warming is higher sea levels.

Effect can be a verb meaning to accomplish: Can the President effect social change with his new law?

3. Allusion and Illusion

    Allusion is a reference: In literature, a dove is an allusion of peace.

    Illusion is a trick: Magicians rely on illusions to trick their audience.

4. Breath and Breathe

    Breath refers to air: On a cold day, you can see your breath.

    Breathe is a verb meaning to inhale or exhale: You must breathe in order to survive.

5. Capital and Capitol

    Capital refers to a place of government: The capital of Maryland is Annapolis.

    Capital also refers to money: He had enough capital to invest in a new restaurant.

    Capitol refers to a building where a legislative body meets: The senators met at the capitol to discuss the upcoming vote on taxes.

6. Conscience and Conscious
    Conscience refers to doing the right thing: His conscience told him to confess to the crime.
    Conscious refers to awareness: A sleeping person is not conscious of the outside world.

7. Compliment and Complement
    Compliment refers to praise as a noun or verb: He complimented her outfit.
    Complement means to go with something: White wine typically complements fish.

8. Emigration and Immigration

Emigration refers to leaving a country: During civil unrest, a country often experiences high emigration rates as civilians flee their homeland.
Immigration refers to entering a country: Many countries experience illegal immigration.

9. Lay and Lie
   Lay means to place an object down: Lay down your weapons and surrender!
   Lie means to recline: If you feel faint, please lie down and rest.
   Lie can also refer to an untruth: Please tell me the truth; I can't stand lies.

10. Lose and Loose
    Lose is the opposite of win: I hope our football team doesn't lose another game.
    Lose also means to misplace: Did you lose your keys again?
    Loose is the opposite of tight: She preferred loose jeans to tight ones.

11. Passed and Past
    Passed is a verb: I passed the semester exam.
    Past refers to a completed event: We can't change the past, but we can change the future.

12. Principal and Principle
    Principal refers to a person: Mr. Rojas is the principal at our high school.
    Principal also means the most important: The principal component of our atmosphere is oxygen.
    Principle refers to a fundamental truth: The United States Constitution is based on a set of principles.

13. Quote and Quotation
    Quote is a verb: She quoted Shakespeare perfectly in her speech.
    Quotation is a noun: Please find ten quotations on the topic of regret.

14. Stationary and Stationery
    Stationary refers to standing still: The guard remained stationary at the front gate.
    Stationery refers to paper: Celia bought some beautiful stationery to write letters to her mother.

15. Than and Then
    Than compares two things: He is faster than a cheetah.
    Then refers to time: I put on my socks then I put on my shoes.

16. Bonus! The most commonly confused abbreviations: i.e. and e.g.
    i.e. hails from the Latin phrase "id est". It means "in other words".
    e.g. hails from the Latin phrase "exempli gratia". It means "for example".

I versus Me

These two pronouns are often confused, especially when writing. To determine which word is appropriate, you may need to rearrange the sentence. Most grammatical errors take place in sentences with a compound subject. Take a look at this example:

- Mark and me are going to the movies.

This shouldn't sound correct to your ear. Listen to the sentence if the words "Mark and" are removed:

- Me is going to the movies.

This sentence definitely doesn't sound correct. Therefore, replace me with I:
- Mark and I are going to the movies.

Fewer verses Less

These two words may seem as though they describe identical instances (i.e. having less of something), however an important distinction exists for these two words. Fewer only describes countable, or tangible, objects. The word less should be used to describe non-countable, or intangible concepts.

- Anna has fewer pets than Mary does.

- If fewer than 50% of shareholders veto the vote, we won't be able to move forward with the merger.

- Mario loved Consuela less than she loved him.

- As an adult, I seem to have less free time than I would like.

Which versus That

These two words are confused a great deal as well. Here's a quick refresher to help you determine when to use each correctly.

Which precedes a relative clause. It can also be used in a sentence that lacks essential qualifiers.

- I love both of these dresses, which one do you think I should buy?

That acts as a restrictive pronoun. A restrictive pronoun's purpose is to introduce essential information that clarifies the information that came before it in the sentence (or the words that came before that).

- I love shopping at farmers' markets that have meats, cheeses, flowers, and produce.

Who versus That

This one is pretty simple. Use who when referring to people. Use that when referring to animals, events, or objects.

- Jeremy is the lifeguard who saved the little girl from drowning yesterday.

- That dog chased my cat up an oak tree!

- The Vietnam War was the war that most damaged the landscape.

- Do you know the store that is having the sale on sunflowers this weekend?

Run-On Sentences

A run-on sentence is exactly what it sounds like: two sentences running together. This common error occurs when a writer fails to properly punctuate the end of a sentence. Run-on sentences may be fixed three different ways, depending upon how the two sentences work together in a text.

1. Christina loved to shop she bought eight new outfits at the mall.

a. Christina loved to shop. She bought eight new outfits at the mall.
   b. Inserting a period correctly separates the two sentences.

2. The weatherman predicts rain today I think it will be sunny.
   a. The weatherman predicts rain today; I think it will be sunny.
   b. A semicolon can connect two independent clauses.

3. My dog loves to run on city sidewalks he is afraid of loud sounds.

   a. My dog loves to run on city sidewalks, but he is afraid of loud sounds.
   b. Connect two independent clauses with a comma and conjunction.

Sentence Fragments

All sentence require a subject and a verb. A subject completes an action, and a verb is the action. The shortest complete sentences are two words: He slept. She won. Sentence fragments are missing one of these key parts; however, they are sometimes difficult to spot because they often have many more than two words.

- The bright, red car. ← Missing a verb. What did the car do?

- The bright, red car sped down the highway.

- Running five miles. ← Missing a subject. Who or what ran five miles?

- Running five miles under an hour was Margaret's best time to date.

Writing Lists Correctly

When writing a list, it's important that the listed items appear in the same form. This is called parallel construction. Just like two parallel lines are identical, the verb tenses or types of phrases describing the items in the list should also be identical.

- Incorrect: I enjoy swimming, running, and being able to hike.

- Correct: I enjoy swimming, running, and hiking.

Parallel construction ensures that a sentence flows well; not only does it sound better to the ear, but it reads better as well.

Who vs. Whom

Who and whom are both pronouns, which means they replace an individual's name in the sentence. Who replaces the subject of a clause, or the person completing an action. Whom replaces the object of a clause, or the person receiving the action.

- Who took my pen? Taylor took my pen.
- Whom will you vote for student president? I will vote for Marcus. (Marcus receives my vote).

CHAPTER 9
Do THIS to Write Better Sentences!

Well-written sentences simply flow. Writing is a tricky business; it's an active business. A writer needs to consciously think about how he or she is using words to ensure that their meaning is properly conveyed. So what are the characteristics of good writing? Whether you're writing a sentence or a paper, the characteristics remain the same:

- Write actively
- Write concisely
- Use strong verbs
- Phrase things positively
- Reduce or eliminate clichés
- Get rid of redundancy
- Eliminate double modifiers

Eventually, once you've got the basics down, you'll be able to turn boring sentences such as "She laughed" into carefully crafted masterpieces such as "Laughter bubbled through her body with pleasure; at first, she felt it in her belly and then she heard it roaring from her lips as if the gods themselves were celebrating the birth of laughter."

Writing Actively

Active sentences capture the reader's attention more readily than passive sentences. Passive constructions are not only wordier, but they make the reader hunt for the sentence's subject. Active sentences place the subject at the front; they are simply easier to follow. Imagine how boring paragraphs would be if they were always written in passive tense:

Julia was loved by Romeo. However, their love was prohibited by their families. Ultimately, this famous play was written about an ongoing feud that ultimately destroyed two families.

- Passive: Friday's presentation will be given by Jack and Jessica.

- Active: Jack and Jessica will present on Friday.

- Jack and Jessica's presentation will be on Friday.

Active sentences are usually shorter than passive sentences. They present information in a more logical format as well since they introduce the "who" and then the "what".

Though most writing should be created in the active voice, the passive voice does have two purposes. First, the passive voice should be used to create suspense. If the writer wishes to withhold the subject, then the passive voice would be appropriate:

- Passive: The body was buried.

If the writer doesn't want the audience to know who buried the body, then he or she should use the passive voice.

Scientific writing also relies a great deal on the passive voice, as this voice allows the writer to recount a specific process.

- Passive: Next, 2 ml of red solution was added to 5 ml of green solution.

Here, the focus is on the process and not on the person. The passive voice is more appropriate in this circumstance.

Writing Concisely

Writing concisely maintains the reader's interest. Better yet, it helps the writer more accurately share his or her purpose for writing. And best of all? Concise writing is short and ultimately saves the writer time! Here are two ways to create more concise sentences.

1. Eliminate Wordy Constructions

2. Many phrases in English may be replaced with shorter, clearer alternatives.

Replace	With

At the present time	Now
At the end of	After
Because of the fact that	Since
Conduct a discussion	Discuss
Due to the fact	Because
Give consideration to	Consider
On a daily basis	Daily
In the event	If
In the future	Soon
In spite of the fact	although
In order to	To
Regardless of the fact that	Although

Other phrases can be eliminated completely without altering the meaning of the sentence:

As a matter of fact…
As far as I'm concerned…
In my opinion…
It is a fact that…
It is clear that…
The point I'm trying to make is…

3. Eliminate Unnecessary Words

   Several common phrases can almost always be eliminated and replaced with better options.

   Of

   If of is being used in a sentence to describe ownership, the sentence should be rewritten in possessive form. For example, "The idea of Brian is good" may be rewritten as "Brian's idea is good."

   There are

   The phrase "there are" may almost always be eliminated from a sentence and replaced. For example, the sentence "There are too many students on this bus." could be rewritten as "This bus holds too many students." or "Too many students entered this bus."

There is

The phrase "there is" is the same as "there are"; it's just the singular version. For example, the sentence "There is one endangered tree left." could be rewritten as "One endangered tree remains."

There were

The phrase "there were" is past tense of "there are". The same logic may be applied to the phrase "there was". For example, the sentence "There were twelve cats in need of a home" could be rewritten as "Twelve cats needed a home."

4. Eliminate redundant phrases

   Several common phrases in English are redundant…meaning that the two words used together mean exactly the same thing. Thankfully, there's a simple fix for redundant phrases: simply choose the better word for your sentence.

   absolutely essential If something is essential, you absolutely need it.

   basic fundamentals Fundamental refers to something that is basic.

   close proximity The word proximity implies that something is close.

   collaborate together If you're collaborating, you're doing something together..

   dollar amount A dollar is an amount

   enter in If you're entering something you're going into it.

   exactly identical If two things are exact, then they are identical.

   foreign imports If something is imported, it is obviously foreign in nature.

   merged together If something is merged, it is already brought together.

new beginning If something is new, it is obviously the beginning

past history If something is considered history, it is already in the past.

protest against If you're protesting something, you're obviously against it.

repeat again If something is repeated, it is happening again.

unexpected surprise If something is a surprise, it was unexpected.

wet rain Rain will always be wet.

Though this list is not comprehensive, it is a good start. When writing, always remember to ask yourself if the phrase you're using could be considered redundant. If so, select the more appropriate word for the context of your paper:

- Original: If we collaborate together, the project will be completed by the deadline.

- Rewritten: By collaborating we'll complete the project by the deadline.

Writing Positively

Writing positively doesn't mean that sentences should only discuss happy subjects; it means that when writing, you should strive to change negative phrasing into positive phrasing. Doing so helps to create clearer sentences. Negatively phrased sentences contain negative words such as not, no, and never.

- Negatively phrased sentence: The dog **was not** sitting still.

- Positively phrased sentence: The dog **ran** around the house.

Positively phrased sentences focus on what the subject is doing. In most instances, the writer should focus on what is happening rather than what is NOT happening in a sentence. When deciding if the negative phrase is important, ask "Is it more important to write what the subject is doing or NOT doing?" In the above example, the focus is on the dog's high energy level; the positively-phrased sentence provides a clearer picture of the dog's high energy.

Writing with Strong Verbs

Just like everything else in life, verbs aren't created equally. Some are simply better than others. Weak verbs lack "umph": is, are, was, were, be, being, been, said, spoke, sit, walk, ask. These are the some of the weakest verbs in the English language. When trying to replace weak verbs with stronger ones, consider how the sentence could be communicated more clearly. You may even ask the verb "How?" in order to determine what stronger verb will work best.

- Weak: Janet **said**, "Of course I'll come with you."

- Strong: Janet whispered, murmured, confided...

- Strong: Janet shouted, begged, yelled, screamed, swore...

- Strong: Janet laughed, chuckled, giggled...

Each of the stronger options conveys *how* Janet said the phrase. The stronger verbs paint a much clearer picture of the situation unfolding for the reader. Using strong verbs helps the writer communicate a more nuanced image for the reader; there is a big difference between begged and laughed. The word begged suggests fear whereas laughed suggests happiness. Therefore, replacing weak verbs with stronger ones helps the reader develop a fuller picture of what's happening in the text.

- Weak: Matthew is experiencing depression often.

- Strong: Matthew battles, experiences, suffers from, struggles with depression.

In this example, replacing "is experiencing" with a stronger verb more clearly conveys how Matthew is dealing with depression. Strong verbs also help the writer create more engaging images. Look at the final example:

- Weak: She is crying.

- Strong: Tears rolled down her face. Sadness enveloped her. She cried for hours. She cried enough tears to fill the Mississippi river.

By asking "How did she cry?", the writer can create levels of meaning—and these levels of meaning help to create a fuller picture regarding the degree of the girl's sadness. Remember: when replacing a weak verb, the sentence may need to be rearranged; words may need to be added, removed, and/or replaced. And that's fine!

Reducing or Eliminating Clichés

Clichés are phrases that are overused; they've been repeated so often that people often tire of hearing them. It's a better idea when writing to create new phrases instead of relying on clichés. If you notice clichés when revising your work, simply brainstorm another way to state your intent. Here are some common clichés that should be avoided when writing:

- All that glitters isn't gold
- Beauty is in the eye of the beholder
- Bend over backwards
- Butterflies in the stomach
- Can't teach an old dog new tricks
- Cold shoulder
- Easy as pie
- Feeling blue
- Hold your horses
- Kiss and tell
- Marches to a different drummer
- My two cents
- Push your (my) buttons
- Put a sock in it

- Read my lips
- The real McCoy
- Rome wasn't built in a day
- Shot in the dark
- Silence is golden
- There's no I in team
- Time after time
- Tongue in cheek
- Waiting for your ship to come in
- Wet behind the ears
- When in Rome
- Wrong side of the tracks
- You can say that again
- Zip it!

In short, people get tired of hearing clichés, so it's a better idea to simply write an original phrase. Here's an example of a revised sentence:

- Cliché: Paul was feeling blue; he hadn't received any birthday cards this year from friends of family.
- Revised: Paul experienced a deep depression after realizing his friends and family had forgotten his birthday.

Getting Rid of Redundancy

Redundancy can manifest several ways in a text. It can appear as the repetition of the same word, similar phrases, synonym pairs, or sentences that echo the same idea without providing any new information. When revising a text, try to eliminate as much repetition as possible.

Word Repetition

Eliminating word repetition is one of the best ways to improve your writing. It allows the writer to create more concise, clearly-written sentences as well as showcase his or her vocabulary. Repetitive word use is one of the quickest ways to lose an audience; readers and listeners often tune out when they hear the same thing over and over and over and over and over…you get the point.

- Redundant: John **hated** spiders. He **hated how they** scurried and **how they** spun **webs**. He especially **hated** walking into **webs**.

- Revised: John hated how spiders scurried and spun webs everywhere he seemed to be walking.

By eliminating the repetition of the words hate, how, they, and webs, the second sentence streamlines the topic and allows the writer to more fully develop the idea of how repulsive John finds spiders.

Similar Phrases

Similar phrases are redundant because the two (or more) words appearing together mean essentially the same thing. Take for example the phrase "absolutely necessary". If something is necessary, it's something you absolutely need; and if it's something you absolutely need, it's something that is necessary. Therefore the phrase "absolutely necessary" is saying the same idea twice. Skip the redundancy and simplify to "necessary".

- Redundant: An effective team collaborates together to accomplish a project to specifications.

- Revised: An effective team collaborates to accomplish a project to specifications.

Eliminating Synonym Pairs

Good writing works to select the best word for each idea it strives to communicate. To accomplish this, writers should avoid using synonym pairs;

instead, writers should select the word that better draws a picture for the reader.

- Redundant: Margaret **feared and dreaded** the annual family reunion.

- Revised: Margaret **dreaded** the annual family reunion.

In the above example, the writer should ask which word more truly describes Margaret's feeling towards the family reunion. Does she fear her family? As in does she believe she may experience mental or physical harm while attending the event? Or is she dreading the event? Does she simply not want to go and spend an afternoon in meaningless chitchat and conversations prying about her personal life?

Synonym pairs will also be connected with "and" or "or". In either case, the writer should select the best word from the pair during the revision process.

Eliminating Echoing Sentences

Echoing sentences are those that repeat the same idea even if the words may be slightly different. Remember the golden rule of writing: respect your audience's time. No doubt you dislike when others waste your time, so kindly remember to honor your audience's time. Communicate your message in the shortest, clearest sentences possible.

- Redundant: Learning to listen is an important skill that takes time to develop. Listening to others is an art form. Once you're able to really hear what others are saying you'll be able to truly connect with them on a deeper level.

- Revised: Listening is a learned skill. When you're able to really hear what others are saying, a connection forms and moves the conversation to a deeper level.

The Revision Process

Sometimes your high school teachers really did know what they were talking about—especially those English teachers. The human brain is a pretty smart organ. It can recognize mistakes and automatically correct them in your head. For instance, it will insert missing words when you're reading so you don't notice a word's absence. This can make the revision process a bit tricky. Revision is kind of like walking: everyone has their own style. However, everyone puts one foot in front of the other to get to their intended destination. To help your brain not only spot but correct grammatical errors, try the following ten helpful hints.

1. Leave yourself enough time to revise.

    Whether it's an office memo or a 20-page report, writers need to set aside the appropriate amount of time to catch errors. You'll be best at catching errors if you're able to walk away from whatever you're writing and look at it with new eyes. Waiting just a few hours can help your brain disengage and then re-engage; however the most effective revisions often occur after several days. It's a good idea to revise longer documents multiple times before submitting them.

2. Get your content straight first.

    Make sure your content is solid first before beginning to critically review your grammar. Because honestly, if what you're saying doesn't make sense, how you're saying it won't matter at all. Really look at whether your ideas are clear. Then look at if you've supported those ideas. Then look at the grammar.

3. Know your weaknesses and revise accordingly.

    If spelling isn't your strong point, then be ready to check questionable words with a print or online dictionary. Spell Check is a great program but it isn't infallible; it will make mistakes. Many writing programs also offer a grammar check. Familiarize yourself with this program and change the settings to benefit you; you can set grammar check to highlight specific grammar issues such as passive voice, redundancy, and verb usage among many others.

4. Revise without distraction.

    Really focus on the task at hand. Turn off the music and work somewhere quiet. The fewer distractions in the immediate environment, the more likely you are to catch any pesky mistakes still lurking in your text. If you can't eliminate distraction, then do your best to work with it. Stay focused with a cup of coffee or healthy snack like trail mix.

5. Print it out.

Although it may seem antiquated, printing out the document and reviewing it with pen-in-hand can help you catch mistakes. Use the pen (or pencil) to point to each word as you review it. This helps your brain actually see what's on the page instead of interpreting what should be there. If it's longer, print double-sided and save some trees.

6. Ask someone else.

    Catching your own mistakes can be difficult because you know what you meant to say; you may impose what you meant to say even if it really isn't there. Asking a trusted friend or coworker to look over an important document will always be a good idea.

7. When in doubt, look it up.

    This may take a few extra seconds, but if you're wondering whether or not you need a comma just conduct a quick search on comma rules and figure it out! Getting it right will always be better than getting it wrong. It's a simple fact that others judge poor grammar—in fact, there are entire internet sites dedicated to posting poor grammatical choices!

8. Know that a better way always exists.

    There will always be a better way to communicate an idea. Really think about what your goal in writing is and how you can make this goal stronger and clearer to your audience. Should you provide more examples of an idea or fewer? Can you create a metaphor to more effectively communicate a process to a client? Can you shorten your report to respect your audience's time while still communicating all the important information? Don't be afraid to try new sentences and delete others.

9. The more you revise, the better you write.

    Here's a secret to revising: the more you do it, the more natural it becomes. It can be a total pain in the beginning. But as you learn and internalize grammar, your brain will automatically begin to arrange sentences without a preposition at the end. You'll actually begin typing good sentences. And then those sentences will become really good.

Putting the time and energy in up front will pay off later. But you've got to commit to the time up front.

10. Demand the best.

    This is true in everything you do. If you accept laziness, you'll be lazy. Demand clarity in your writing and you'll do it. Think of grammar as your friend; if you think of it as your enemy writing will always be a warzone! Good grammar allows you to communicate exactly what you intend to your audience.

CHAPTER 10
Notes on Good Writing (You Can Do It, Trust Me!)

Well-written documents are sometimes hard to come by…anyone can publish anything they wish online. And while this sometimes makes wading through poorly-written articles online a monumental task, it makes readers appreciate well-written articles and documents all that much more. So what are the characteristics of good writing? That's a great question. Here are eleven good answers.

1. Master Parallel Structure

   This writing technique isn't just for paragraphs or essays; it also strengthens resumes, white papers, and pretty much any form of personal or professional communication. Not only does parallel structure ensure grammatical agreement, but it also improves the flow of ideas.

2. Include Sentence Variety

   No one wants to eat the exact same meal every day. The same is true for what people want to read. The audience expects variety—not only in the sentence's purpose, but in the sentence's form as well. When reviewing drafts of your work, quickly asses the ratio of simple, complex, and compound-complex sentences. Try to mix up the ratio to ensure diversity in your writing.

3. Check Spelling

   Computers aren't perfect. Although many spelling programs will catch a lot of errors, they won't catch all of them. Indeed, many homophones may fall through the cracks. It's a good idea to print out your paper, highlight any words you're unsure of and double check them against a dictionary (online or print) before handing in your paper.

4. Write in Complete Sentences

   It's true that sentence fragments and run-ons have a purpose; however, most writing requires complete sentences. Learning to identify and correct both of these sentence errors not only saves you time, but saves you face. Just make sure that all your sentences have a clear subject and verb.

5. Use Grammar Check

    Most Word programs offer a fairly thorough grammar check program. Though not infallible, these programs are pretty good at catching a variety of grammatical issues ranging from fragments to passive voice. Go into the grammar check's settings and help the program really work for you.

6. Following Formatting Guidelines

    Different writing forms demand different organization. Learn the formats or know where to find reliable information to help you. Follow your teacher's or boss's instructions when writing for a specific audience.

7. Funnel Your Paragraphs

    The sole purpose of a paragraph is to support a single idea. Each new idea requires a new paragraph. A well-written paragraph should mimic the shape of a funnel: broad at the top and narrow at the bottom. Begin with a topic sentence and supply supporting sentences until the idea is substantiated. Then, move on.

8. Know Your Purpose

    Badly-written articles simply seem to wander. The audience is never quite sure where they're going because the writer seems unable to follow a clear path. Brainstorm, organize, and then refine your purpose.

9. Consciously Choose Words

    Good words will make all the difference. Demonstrate the range of your vocabulary be eliminating repetition and really striving to select the best possible words and phrases to communicate your idea to the audience.

10. Evaluate Credibility

    This applies not only to the primary and secondary sources within a piece, but to the writer as well. What will make the audience trust you as the author? How can you establish yourself as an authority? If you aren't an authority, are you using the best available resources to support your ideas?

11. Revise Again

    Revision is a process for a reason: it requires multiple attempts to get it right. Few things exist in life that are perfect the first time around; writing is no different. The more you really look at your writing, the more you'll be able to fine tune it to accomplish its task. Leave enough time to review simple issues such as spelling and grammar and larger issues such as organization and flow.

CHAPTER 11
Writing Formats (These Can Be Confusing...)

Two basic categories of writing exist: informal and formal. Informal writing includes writing of a personal nature that may or may not be edited. Writing such as emails between friends and family, letters, and journals or diaries all fall into this category. Informal writing is often full of personal opinions, slang words, and grammatically incorrect sentences. It may or may not be published.

Formal writing encompasses a much larger body of writing; it's so much larger in fact that there are several subcategories to help group the different kinds of writing. The five subcategories include expository writing, descriptive writing, narrative writing, creative writing, and persuasive writing.

Expository Writing

Expository writing focuses on informing or defining a subject for the audience. Research reports, textbooks, and literary analysis all fall into this category as do some magazine, newspaper, and online articles. This type of writing is void of personal opinions because it strives to provide only factual and supported theories to the audience. Expository pieces rely on quoted material and generally cite several sources to support a thesis or topic.

Descriptive Writing

This type of writing includes formats whose focus is on developing visuals for the audience. Descriptive writing may aim to depict a real, historic event or a fictional, futuristic event. This form of writing nearly always relies heavily upon literary devices such as metaphors, similes, allusions, and imagery (to name a few). In addition, descriptive writing focuses on the five senses: sight, sound, taste, smell, and touch. Though it can be entirely used in isolation, descriptive writing is often paired with other writing formats to strengthen their appeal to an audience.

Narrative Writing

This writing type centers on telling a story. It may be a true story, such as an autobiography or biography, or a fictional piece, such as a mystery, horror, or science-fiction story. Generally, a character or small group of characters reveals the story over the course of the short story or novel. All narrative writing includes a plot as well as other various narrative devices such as conflict and characterization.

Creative Writing

Though some narrative writing may also be considered creative writing, most creative writing is not considered narrative writing. Creative writing is considered the most enjoyable form of writing because it lacks the rules that other forms of writing follow. This writing form includes plays, poetry, short stories, novellas, and novels. Creative non-fiction can also fall into this category.

Persuasive Writing

Persuasive writing aims to sway the audience. Simply put, this writing form states an opinion and works to persuade the audience to embrace the writer's argument. Advertisements (written and auditory) rely heavily on persuasive writing to entice their audience to purchase a particular product. Op-Ed, or Opinion Editorials, in newspapers are a great example of persuasive writing.

Now that you've got the types of writing down, let's take a look at different writing formats. So what is a writing format? A format refers to a specific expectation. For example, there's a big difference between writing a personal essay for college and writing a short story. Though both may be two pages in length, the written content within both pieces should be vastly different. It's important to remember that some formats may blend types of writing. Let's take a look at a few common writing formats.

Abstracts

An abstract is a short summative statement mainly used for scientific papers or literary analysis. This is a short piece of writing, typically a single paragraph though they can be longer. It provides answers to the who, what, when, where, and how questions. Abstracts should present information as it appears in the paper or analysis. This writing form should not be the conclusion paragraph; it should be a stand-alone document. Abstracts often have word limits, and it is important to adhere to any limits given.

Articles

Articles are short pieces that may appear in various publications including newspapers, magazines, and the internet. They should have a title and by-line prior to the text. This writing format is typically several paragraphs and may range from a single page to multiple pages in length. Article writing generally focuses on non-fiction elements and may range from the serious to the satirical. A brief author bio may or may not appear after the article's conclusion.

Business Letter

A business letter may be written from an individual to a business or a business to a business. Standard formatting exists which a writer should always follow. If available, business letters should be typed on letterhead. If letterhead with the sender's address is not available, then the letter should begin by placing the sender's address (just street, city, and zip code) at the top left. Next, write the date. The inside address comes next. A full address, beginning with a specific individual at the business you're writing to should come next. Skip several lines and add a salutation. The salutations should be formal and include a person's title. Salutations should be followed by a colon (Dear Mrs. Turnbow:). Skip a line and begin the body of the letter. The body may be a single paragraph or several paragraphs. When finished writing, add a closing that aligns vertically with the date. A comma should follow the closing word or phrase. Remember to leave space to sign your name! If including enclosures, such as a resume or other documents, type the word Enclosures after the space left for the writer's signature. It is customary to list the title of each enclosed document.

Editorials

Editorials are a type of article that appear in newspapers. They are a biased form of writing; they aim to persuade readers about a specific issue. The goal of editorials is to engage the reader in an important debate and encourage him or her to take action. This form of writing can be written by a single individual or by a group at a newspaper. An editorial is usually unsigned.

Essays

Essays are relatively short pieces that present a singular idea and support it. Their focus may range from merely discussing a topic, such as the beauty of daffodils, to analyzing an idea such as why dogs make the best pets. Because essay topics are so wide-ranging, there are many types of essays. Here are the eight most common essays you may come across:

1. Argumentative

As its name suggests, an argumentative essay presents an argument to the reader. It's important to remember that the argument is not personal in nature; the writer is simply presenting a statement and providing evidence regarding the position of the essay. This essay must begin by clearly conveying a debatable point and working to prove the essay's thesis. Though typically serious in nature, argumentative essays can also be comedic.

2. Cause and Effect

    Though generally used in the science and business worlds, cause and effect essays can be a staple in literary realms as well. This essay form focuses on identifying the cause of an event and describing the effects of the event. For example, a history professor may assign an essay on the cause and effects of WWII while an ecology professor may assign an essay on the cause and effects of rising oceanic temperatures on the global ecosystem. Cause and effect essays are typically structured by identifying the cause in the opening paragraph(s) and then discussing each effect in a separate paragraph.

3. Compare and Contrast

    As its title suggests, a compare and contrast essay aims to highlight commonalities and differences between two or more items. This essay is a favorite of nearly all disciplines, as a writer could compare and contrast two poets, two mathematical concepts, two scientific processes...the list is endless. This essay form should be devoid of personal bias and focus solely on presenting facts. Compare and contrast essays may be structured several ways; however, the most common method of organization involves an introduction, separate paragraphs for each commonality and difference, and a discussion paragraph which analyzes how the similarities and differences affect the topic.

4. Critical

    A critical essay may also be referred to as an analysis essay. This essay form aims to examine the how or why of a topic. Most often critical essays examine the reasons behind an author's choice in a literary work. These essays rely heavily on quotations and primary source material. Typically, critical essays begin by identifying the strengths and weaknesses of a literary work and then continue by discussing whether or not the author met his or her goal by the end of the work.

5. Definition

    This essay focuses on defining a particular idea. Oftentimes, this idea relates to an abstract concept. A definition essay doesn't aim to merely provide a denotative definition; it aims to provide a comprehensive definition of a complicated concept. For example, an appropriate topic for this essay form would be "What is art?" or "How do people define family?" Though a definition essay may be a single, long paragraph, these essays are typically multiple paragraphs.

6. Descriptive

    This essay aims to fully describe a singular idea using sensory details. Descriptive essays tend to focus on describing personal experiences. For example, topics may include a writer's favorite vacation spot, or sharing the love of a particular plant. By providing specific details regarding sight, smell, taste, touch, and sound a reader more fully visualizes what the writer attempts to describe in the essay. Like definition essays, description essays may be a singular paragraph; however, they can be divided into multiple paragraphs. Many times, writers may choose to organize their paragraphs by sense.

7. Narrative

    This essay shares a story. Its sole purpose is to relate a personal experience, so personal pronouns such as I, me, my, we, and our are appropriate. Although these essays typically share a teachable moment, they may also share a simple moment in time. They are usually multi-paragraph and arranged chronologically.

8. Process

    Process essays are often referred to as "How-to" essays. This type of essay shares the steps a reader must take to accomplish a certain task. Though most common in scientific disciplines, process essays can also be written from a personal standpoint; therefore, their topics may range from how to correctly identify to monarch butterfly to how to survive planning a wedding. It is important to consider the audience when writing a process essay. For example, if the topic of the essay was "How to Butcher a Chicken", the amount of detail and vocabulary would vary greatly if the audience was a group of amateur chefs rather than professional chefs.

Executive Summary

This writing format is similar to an abstract but longer. Executive summaries are usually a page long and focus on stating the problem discussed within a report, highlighting why the report was necessary, and reviewing relevant conclusions as well as recommendations.

Letter to the Editor

This specific letter is written by a reader to the editor of a newspaper or other publication. It may compliment or criticize a story run by the newspaper; it may also bring an uncovered story to light important to the local community. Letters to the Editor are very concise and focus on a singular point. They are often short and focus on factual evidence regarding a topic. They are usually signed.

Memo

A memo is a short piece of writing used to inform the reader of an action. It may be an action the reader needs to take such as attending a workshop, or an action the company is taking that will impact employees. Memos should be short and to the point. Though they can be longer, memos are usually a short paragraph.

The Paragraph

A well-written paragraph is key to nearly all forms of writing. All paragraphs should have the following elements: a strong topic sentence, support sentences, and a conclusion. Though the topic sentence is often the first sentence, it doesn't have to be—especially if the paragraph begins with an attention getting sentence to capture the reader's interest. After stating the topic sentence, every following sentence should work to support the topic sentence. If a sentence fails to support the claim within the topic sentence, it should be eliminated. Within a paragraph, a writer should use transitional words such as first, second, next, now, and another to connect ideas and strengthen sentence flow.

The Five-Paragraph Essay

A favorite in academia, the five-paragraph essay follows a very specific format: introduction paragraph, three body paragraphs, a conclusion paragraph. The introduction paragraph provides background information as well as a thesis statement. The thesis statement typically consists of three supporting ideas, each which become topic sentences in the body paragraphs. For example, a simple thesis statement could be Cats make the best pets because they are intelligent, playful, and clean. After providing background information on cats as pets, the writer would support the claim that they make the best pets by writing a paragraph providing evidence of their intelligence, a second providing evidence on how they are playful, and a third providing evidence on how they are clean. Finally, in the conclusion paragraph the writer reviews the strength of his or her argument and ends the paper. Conclusion paragraphs should never introduce new material.

Personal Journal

This writing form has the least formatting guidelines. Personal journals may be written purely for the enjoyment of capturing one's thoughts or they may be a classroom requirement. If the latter is true, it's important to remember your audience and censor writing as appropriate. This writing format enjoys the freedom of writing however the writer would like; personal journals may appear as paragraphs, lists, poems, vignettes, or any combination.

Research Paper

This writing form focuses on gathering credible sources to support a specific topic. Two types of research papers exist: argumentative and analytical. Argumentative papers state a position and provide evidence to prove the writer's claim. For example, an argumentative paper may judge the role of U.S. banks in the global financial crisis. An analytical paper presents research that investigates a particular issue. For example, this type of paper may examine the historical significance of the Pony Express.

Because research papers may be written within many disciplines, several formats exists to help organize information within a research paper—especially information for citations. Before beginning a research paper, it is very important that the writer know which style the paper should adhere to. The three most common research formats include MLA (Modern Language Association), APA (American Psychological Association), and the Chicago Manual of Style. Each of these formats discusses specific guidelines regarding titles, page formats, citations, bibliography pages and works referenced pages.

White Paper

White papers are used in the professional world to present a position and support it; in other words, this writing form advocates for a particular direction. For example, a company may create a white paper to outline the best branding strategy for a new product. While white papers help companies visualize a new direction, they can also persuade consumers about the necessity of a product. Companies may publish white papers to address consumer needs. This writing format is organized like a report: it states the goal and provides evidence regarding how a product or idea will meet the goal.

CHAPTER 12
5 Amazing Grammar Websites to Supercharge Your Learning

This book provides only the basics concerning grammar rules—essential information to be sure, but English is a complicated language. In other words, it's a great start, but the information provided here is by no means a comprehensive guide to the ins and outs of grammar. If you find yourself needing a bit more information than these 50-plus pages offer, consider heading to one of these great grammar websites.

1. Purdue University's Online Writing Lab

    This is an excellent resource for both students and professionals. They break down and clearly explain concepts and provide multiple examples to demonstrate how to apply grammar rules correctly in a sentence. Beyond general writing guidelines, they also offer specific help on research and citation methods as well as subject-specific writing (everything from academic writing to creative writing to writing in specific fields such as engineering, medical, and nursing). And if you're a visual and/or auditory learner, they also offer a variety of their lessons as "Vidcasts" on their YouTube channel.

2. Grammarly

    This website can "instantly find and correct over 250 types of grammatical mistakes". If you don't have a second (or third) set of eyes to review your work, then head over here. Another benefit Grammarly provides is a plagiarism check; this website will check your document against more than 8 billion internet sites to ensure your work contains original content. Although a small trial is free, Grammarly requires payment. However it will find mistakes that Word programs miss. It's worth the price.

3. Daily Grammar

    Created by a 30-year veteran teacher, this website offers free, daily grammar lessons through its blog as well as additional materials to purchase. It's online glossary is a great resource to help demystify many grammatical terms such as interrogative pronouns, objective complement, and predicate nominative. Each glossary term is linked to the lesson(s) that further clarify that particular grammatical concept or term.

4. Guide to Grammar and Writing

    This site provides extensive information broken into four main sections: word and sentences, paragraphs, and essays and research papers. Each section contains a drop-down menu with dozens of specific lessons to help a writer achieve his or her goal. In addition, the site offers PowerPoint tutorials as well as other online resources to help writers.

5. Grammar Bytes

    This is more of a fun site. Its Terms page offers users a short but sweet definition of grammar terms as well as examples. Several terms even have their own YouTube videos. Visitors can even test their grammatical knowledge with interactive exercises on 11 common grammar mistakes. If you're curious if you really understand grammar and how to use it, take several of interactive quizzes—you'll quickly be able to identify your strengths and weaknesses as a writer.

CHAPTER 13
Congratulations, You've Done It! - Where to Go From Here

Well, you can't apply the rules of grammar without actually writing…so pick up that pen and put it to paper or sit in a quiet spot and start typing. It doesn't matter if you must write a report for work, a final paper for a class, or a story just for yourself: you have to begin. Remember the metaphor about writing and walking? Well it's perfect. Although a writing task may seem daunting, you simply need to write one word, one sentence, one paragraph at a time. Leave yourself enough time to adequately finish a project—set aside the time to brainstorm, to write, and finally to revise (and revise again).

Here's the trick to good writing: sit down and write. Don't worry about revision until you're finished. Get all the ideas down first, then worry about shaping them into the best possible ideas they can be. You can add the finesse and the grammatically correct elements later.

Good writers write well on their own. Great writers rely on the eyes of others to catch those pesky things that they might miss. So when the writing is complete and you've altered it to the best of your ability, hand it to someone else to look at; he or she just may help you make it even better.

If you're in high school, ask an English teacher. If you're in college, ask a peer or use the campus writing center. If you're a working professional, ask a trusted colleague or friend. Plenty of individuals out there are willing to help—however, you must ask first. And don't forget to respect your reviewer's time. If you hand him or her a finished project with a deadline of 24 hours, your reviewer won't be able to really review your writing. Allocate the proper amount of time according to the length of the writing. A short but important memo may only need a day but a ten to twenty page report needs several days.

One of the easiest ways to learn good grammar is by reading. Read novels and magazines and newspapers. The more professional writing you read the more you'll see good grammar in action. Your brain will simply internalize well-written sentences and eventually it will pass on the traits of good writing to you. The more you read, the more sentences and paragraphs you will be exposed to, and this exposure allows your brain to expand its knowledge. The greater the knowledge base, the better your own writing will become. Find a few writers you enjoy and just devour their work. Read a little every day. Whether you choose fiction or non-fiction is irrelevant; choose something you're interested in…and simply read.

Perhaps the most important reason for learning and applying correct grammar is that it is in fact what separates us from other animals. Sure, other animals can communicate vocally. Some animals such as elephants, dolphins, and gorillas have highly developed language. However, humans are the only living thing on earth that have a written system of communication. Therefore, grammar exists as a defining characteristic of our species. Even those animals with developed verbal communication can't *write*. Noam Chomsky said it best:

> It's perfectly obvious that there is some genetic factor that distinguishes humans from other animals and that it is language-specific. The theory of that genetic component, whatever it turns out to be, is what is called universal grammar.

So where should you go from here? You should stop procrastinating. You should master grammar. You should write. And you should write well.

To your success!

Dagny Taggart

Preview Of "Learn Spanish In 7 DAYS! - The Ultimate Crash Course To Learn The Basics of the Spanish Language In No Time"

Are You ready? It's Time To Learn Spanish!

Most people are daunted by the idea of learning a language. They think it's impossible, even unfathomable. I remember as a junior in high school, watching footage of Jackie O giving a speech in French. I was so impressed and inspired by the ease at which she spoke this other language of which I could not understand one single word.

At that moment, I knew I had to learn at least one foreign language. I started with Spanish, later took on Mandarin, and most recently have started learning Portuguese. No matter how challenging and unattainable it may seem, millions of people have done it. You do NOT have to be a genius to learn another language. You DO have to be willing to take risks and make mistakes, sometimes even make a fool of yourself, be dedicated, and of course, practice, practice, practice!

This book will only provide you with the basics in order to get started learning the Spanish language. It is geared towards those who are planning to travel to a Spanish-speaking country and covers many common scenarios you may find yourself in so feel free to skip around to the topic that is most prudent to you at the moment. It is also focused on the Spanish of Latin America rather than Spain. Keep in mind, every Spanish-speaking country has some language details specific to them so it would be essential to do some research on the specific country or countries that you will visit.

I will now list some tips that I have found useful and should be very helpful to you in your journey of learning Spanish. I don't wish you luck because that will not get you anywhere- reading this book, dedicating yourself, and taking some risks will!

Important note

Due to the nature of this book (it contains charts, graphs, and so on), you will better your reading experience by setting your device on *LANDSCAPE* mode!

Language Tips

Tip #1 - Keep an Open Mind

It may seem obvious but you must understand that languages are very different from each other. You cannot expect them to translate word for word. *'There is a black dog'* will not translate word for word with the same word order in Spanish. You have to get used to the idea of translating WHOLE ideas. So don't find yourself saying, *"Why is everything backwards in Spanish?"* because it may seem that way many times. Keep your mind open to the many differences that you will find in the language that go far beyond just the words.

Tip #2 - Take Risks

Be fearless. Talk to as many people as you can. The more practice you get the better and don't worry about looking like a fool when you say, *"I am pregnant"* rather than *"I am embarrassed,"* which as you will find out can be a common mistake. If anyone is laughing remember they are not laughing at you. Just laugh with them, move on, and LEARN from it, which brings us to our next tip.

Tip #3 - Learn from your Mistakes

It doesn't help to get down because you made one more mistake when trying to order at a restaurant, take a taxi, or just in a friendly conversation. Making mistakes is a HUGE part of learning a language. You have to put yourself out there as we said and be willing to make tons of mistakes! Why? Because what can you do with mistakes. You can LEARN from them. If you never make a mistake, you probably are not learning as much as you could. So every time you mess up when trying to communicate, learn from it, move on, and keep your head up!

Tip #4 - Immerse yourself in the language

If you're not yet able to go to a Spanish-speaking country, try to pretend that you are. Surround yourself with Spanish. Listen to music in Spanish, watch movies, TV shows, in Spanish. Play games on your phone, computer, etc. in Spanish. Another great idea is to actually put your phone, computer, tablet and/or other electronic devices in Spanish. It can be frustrating at first but in the end this exposure will definitely pay off.

Tip #5 - Start Thinking in Spanish

I remember being a senior in high school and working as a lifeguard at a fairly deserted pool. While I was sitting and staring at the empty waters, I would speak to myself or think to myself (to not seem so crazy) in Spanish. I would describe my surroundings, talk about what I had done and what I was going to do, etc. While I was riding my bike, I would do the same thing. During any activity when you don't need to talk or think about anything else, keep your brain constantly going in Spanish to get even more practice in the language. So get ready to turn off the English and jumpstart your Spanish brain!

Tip #6 - Label your Surroundings/Use Flashcards

When I started to learn Portuguese, I bought an excellent book that included stickers so that you could label your surroundings. So I had stickers all over my parents' house from the kitchen to the bathroom that labeled the door, the dishes, furniture, parts of the house, etc. It was a great, constant reminder of how to say these objects in another language. You can just make your own labels and stick them all over the house and hope it doesn't bother your family or housemates too much!

Tip #7 - Use Context clues, visuals, gestures, expressions, etc.

If you don't understand a word that you have heard or read, look or listen to the surrounding words and the situation to help you. If you are in a restaurant and your friend says, "I am going to ??? a sandwich." You can take a guess that she said *order* or *eat* but you don't have to understand every word in order to understand the general meaning. When you are in a conversation use gestures, expressions, and things around you to help communicate your meaning. Teaching English as a second language to young learners taught me this. If you act everything out, you are more likely to get your point across. If you need to say the word *bird* and you don't know how you can start flapping your arms and chirping and then you will get your point across and possibly learn how to say *bird*. It may seem ridiculous but as I said, you have to be willing to look silly to learn another language and this greatly helps your language communication and learning.

Tip #8 - Circumlocution

Circumlo… what? This is just a fancy word for describing something when you don't know how to say it. If you are looking to buy an umbrella and don't know how to say it, what can you do? You can describe it using words you know. You can say, it is something used for the rain that opens and closes and then hopefully someone will understand you, help you, and maybe teach you how to say this word. Using circumlocution is excellent language practice and is much better than just giving up when you don't know how to say a word. So keep talking even if you have a limited vocabulary. Say what you can and describe or act out what you can't!

SECTION 1: THE BASICS

Chapter 1: Getting the Pronunciation Down

Below I will break down general Spanish pronunciation for the whole alphabet dividing it into vowels and consonants. One great thing about Spanish is that the letters almost always stay consistent as far as what sound they make. Unlike English in which the vowels can make up to 27 different sounds depending on how they are mixed. Be thankful that you don't have to learn English or at least have already learned English. There are of course some sounds in Spanish that we never make in English and you possibly have never made in your life. So get ready to start moving your mouth and tongue in a new way that may seem strange at first but as I keep saying, practice makes perfect!

The charts on the next page will explain how to say the letter, pronounce it, and if there is an example in an English word of how to say it I put it in the right column.

Vowel Sounds

Vowel	How to say the letter	How to pronounce it in a word	As in…
a	Ah	Ah	Taco
e	Eh	Eh	Egg
i	Ee	Ee	Easy
o	Oh	Oh	Open
u	Oo	Oo	Book

Consonant Sounds

Consonant	How to say the letter	How to pronounce it in a word	As in…
b	beh	similar to English b	
c	ceh	k after *a, o,* or *u* s after *e* or *i*	cat cereal
ch	cheh	ch	cheese
d	deh	a soft d (place your tongue at the back of your upper teeth)	three
f	efe	F	free
g	geh	h before i or e g before a, o, u	him go
h	ache	silent	

j	hota	H	him
k	kah	K	karaoke
l	ele	like English l with tongue raised to roof of mouth	
ll	eye	Y	yes
m	eme	M	money
n	ene	N	no
ñ	enye	Ny	canyon
p	peh	like English p but you don't aspirate	

Consonants continued

Consonant	How to say the letter	How to pronounce it in a word	As in...
Q	koo	k (q is always followed by u like English)	quilt
R	ere	* at the beginning of a word you must roll your r's by vibrating tongue at roof of mouth * in the middle of a word it sounds like a soft d	
rr	erre	roll your r's as mentioned above	
S	ese	Like English s	sorry
T	teh	a soft English t, the tongue touches the back of the upper teeth	
V	veh	like Spanish b	boots

Consonants continued

Consonant	How to say the letter	How to pronounce it in a word	As in...
w	dobleveh	like English w	water
x	equis	*Between vowels and at the end of a word, it sounds like the English ks. *At the beginning of a word, it sounds like the letter s.	*box *sorry
y	igriega	like English y	yellow
z	seta	s	six

Note: If you're not sure how to pronounce a word, one thing you can do is type it in *Google translate* then click on the little speaker icon in the bottom left corner to hear the correct pronunciation.

To check out the rest of " Learn Spanish In 7 DAYS! - The Ultimate Crash Course To Learning The Basics of The Spanish Language In No Time", **go to Amazon and look for it right now!**

Ps: You'll find many more books like these under my name, Dagny Taggart. Don't miss them! Here's a short list:

- Learn **Spanish** In 7 Days!
- Learn **French** In 7 Days!
- Learn **German** In 7 Days!
- Learn **Italian** In 7 Days!
- Learn **Portuguese** In 7 Days!

- Learn **Japanese** In 7 Days!
- Learn **Chinese** In 7 Days!

- Learn **Russian** In 7 Days!

- Learn Any Language FAST!

- How to Drop Everything & Travel Around The World

About the Author

Dagny Taggart is a language enthusiast and polyglot who travels the world, inevitably picking up more and more languages along the way.

Taggart's true passion became learning languages after she realized the incredible connections with people that it fostered. Now she just can't get enough of it. Although it's taken time, she has acquired vast knowledge on the best and fastest ways to learn languages. But the truth is, she is driven simply by her motive to build exceptional links and bonds with others.

She is inspired everyday by the individuals she meets across the globe. For her, there's simply not anything as rewarding as practicing languages with others because she gets to make friends with people from all that come from a variety of cultures. This, in turn, has broadened her mind and thinking more than she would have ever imagined it could.

Of course, as a result of her constant travels, Taggart has become an expert on planning trips and making the most of time spent out of what she calls her "base" town. She jokes that she's practically at the nomad status now, but she's more content to live that way.

She knows how to live on a manageable budget weather she's in Paris or Phnom Penh. She knows how to seek out the adventures and thrills, no doubt, lying in wait at any city she visits. She knows that reflection on each every experience is significant if she wants to grow as a traveler and student of the world's cultures.

Because of this, Taggart chooses to share her understanding of languages and travel so that others, too, can experience the same life-altering benefits she has.

Printed in Great Britain
by Amazon.co.uk, Ltd.,
Marston Gate.